100

cookies

from 1 easy recipe

100 cookies

from 1 easy recipe

Linda Doeser

This edition published in 2012
LOVE FOOD is an imprint of Parragon Books Ltd

Parragon
Queen Street House
4 Queen Street
Bath BA1 1HE, UK

www.parragon.com

ISBN: 978-1-4454-7081-8

Printed in China

Cover design by Talking Design
Written by Linda Doeser
Internal design by Simon Levy
Photography by Clive Streeter
Home economy by Angela Drakes, Teresa Goldfinch and Carole Streeter

Notes for the Reader
This book uses standard kitchen measuring spoons and cups. All spoon
and cup measurements are level unless otherwise indicated. Unless
otherwise stated, milk is assumed to be whole, eggs are large, individual
vegetables are medium, and pepper is freshly ground black pepper.

The times given are only an approximate guide. Preparation times differ
according to the techniques used by different people and the cooking
times may also vary from those given. Optional ingredients, variations,
or serving suggestions have not been included in the calculations.

Recipes using raw or very lightly cooked eggs should be avoided by
infants, the elderly, pregnant women, convalescents, and anyone with a
chronic illness. Pregnant and breast-feeding women are advised to avoid
eating peanuts and peanut products. People with nut allergies should be
aware that some of the prepared ingredients used in the recipes in this
book may contain nuts. Always check the packaging before use.

Contents

6 Introduction

12 Gooey

54 Crunch

96 Party

140 Fruity

182 Double the Fun

222 Index

Introduction

Whether we're desperate for a well-earned, mid-morning cup of coffee or the kids have come home from school too ravenous to wait until dinner time, cookies will invariably hit the spot. Sometimes, we just want to congratulate ourselves with a little self-indulgent treat, at others we require a subtle accompaniment to a spectacular dinner party dessert. Equally, we might want to make a colorful, fun snack for a child's birthday or to bake edible decorations for the Christmas tree.

The great thing about homemade cookies—apart from the fact that they taste terrific—is that they are quick and easy to make and astonishingly versatile. There are recipes for one hundred different cookies in this book, ranging from wonderfully sticky and rich chocolate treats to crisp and crunchy snacks, and from positively sinful nibbles with cocktail-flavored frosting to fruit- and-nut filled delights. Every one of these is a variation of a single Basic Cookie Dough (see page 10). How simple is that?

Equipment

You won't need to buy any expensive or special kitchen tools. In fact, you probably already have most of what's required— measuring cups and spoons, mixing bowls, wooden spoons, chopping knives, whisks, spatula, rolling pin, and a sieve.

If you're going to make a lot of cookies—and once you've started, it's hard to resist the temptation to bake more—it's worth buying good-quality, nonstick cookie sheets. However, cookie sheets that do not have a nonstick coating can simply be lined with baking parchment. Before buying new cookie sheets, check the dimensions of your oven to make sure they will fit.

Baking parchment, which has a shiny, nonstick surface, is useful in a number of ways. When rolling out cookie dough, it's better to put the dough between two sheets of baking parchment than to dust the counter with flour. This is because even a little flour can affect the texture and appearance of the cookies. Some decorated cookies and candied flowers and fruit are best left to dry on a sheet of baking parchment.

One or more wire racks is essential when the cookies are cooling, because the design lets air circulate, thus preventing the cookies from becoming soggy. They are available in different shapes and sizes.

You will probably already have cookie cutters, but there is such a range of shapes and sizes that you might be tempted to buy some more, particularly for festive cookies or special occasions. Some of the cutters available include plain and fluted rounds, hearts, stars, crescents, snowflakes, numbers, alphabet, squares, rectangles, holly leaves, Christmas trees, and even Santa Claus—not to mention gingerbread and teddy bear families. Metal cutters are better than plastic, because they don't compress the edges of the cookies.

You will find that there are many ways to decorate cookies without needing a pastry bag. However, a medium-sized bag, preferably double stitched for strength, and a selection of tips won't break the bank and might inspire your creative instincts. As the decoration on cookies is less elaborate than on cakes, a small plastic bag with the corner snipped off is often all that's required.

Ingredients

Butter is the ideal fat for making cookies, giving them a rich flavor that margarine can't match. As the Basic Cookie Dough recipe in this book involves creaming the butter with the sugar, remove the butter from the refrigerator in advance to allow time for it to soften slightly.

Superfine sugar is the type most frequently used for making cookies because the grains are very fine and it combines easily with the other ingredients. It is also used for sprinkling over freshly baked cookies. Some recipes specify golden superfine sugar, which has exactly the same qualities as white sugar but provides extra color. Superfine sugar may be flavored in a variety of ways. The most common method is to put a vanilla bean in a jar of sugar and leave it for about a week. An unusual and aromatic flavor is produced by putting rose petals in a jar of sugar. Make sure that they are fresh, dry, disease-free, and have not been sprayed with chemicals.

Confectioners' sugar is powdery and used to make frostings and buttercream fillings. It can also be dusted over cookies to decorate. It should always be sifted first.

Coffee, turbinado, and granulated sugars may all be used to decorate cookies.

The flour used in the Basic Cookie Dough recipe in this book is all-purpose flour and it should be sifted even if it is labeled that it has already been sifted.

Egg yolk is used to bind the dry ingredients together and it also helps to enrich the dough. Remove eggs from the refrigerator in advance to let them come to room temperature. You can use an egg separator to separate the yolk from the white or just tip the whole egg into your hand and allow the white to drain through your fingers. A less messy way is to crack the shell and pry it apart, then let the white drain into a bowl while retaining the yolk in a half shell. Tip the yolk into the other half shell to let the remaining white drain.

Various aromatic extracts are available, the most commonly used being vanilla, which goes well with a lot of other flavors, including chocolate. Others used in this book include almond, orange, and peppermint. When buying, check the labels carefully to avoid artificial flavorings.

A huge range of dried fruits is available nowadays, from classic vine fruits, such as currants, to exotic varieties, such as papaya. Both dried and candied fruits are great for flavoring cookies.

Nuts are a popular flavoring and also add texture to cookies. They may be used whole, chopped, or ground and can feature as decoration as well as forming part of the dough. Nuts cannot be stored for very long, so buy them in small quantities and keep in an airtight container.

Semisweet, bittersweet, milk, and white chocolate feature in both cookie dough and cookie decorations, whether chopped, grated, melted, or in the form of chocolate chips or chocolate sprinkles. Good-quality, sifted unsweetened cocoa powder also provides a rich chocolate flavor to the dough and can be dusted over baked cookies.

Basic Cookie Dough

Makes about 30

* ✳ 2 cups butter, softened
* ✳ scant ¾ cup superfine sugar
* ✳ 1 egg yolk, lightly beaten
* ✳ 2 tsp vanilla extract
* ✳ 2½ cups all-purpose flour
* ✳ salt

This is the recipe that all 100 variations of cookie in the book are based on.

For each recipe the basic mix is highlighted (✳) for easy reference, so then all you have to do is follow the easy steps each time and a world of delicious and delectable cookies will await you.

Please note the basic ingredients may vary from time to time, so please check these carefully.

Gooey

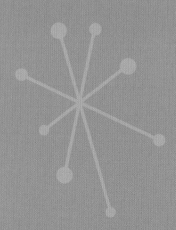

Double Choc Cookies

1. Preheat the oven to 375°F/190°C. Line 2 cookie sheets with baking parchment.

2. Put the butter and sugar into a bowl and mix well with a wooden spoon, then beat in the egg yolk and vanilla extract. Sift together the flour, unsweetened cocoa, and a pinch of salt into the mixture, add the chopped chocolate and sour cherries, and stir until thoroughly combined.

3. Scoop up tablespoons of the mixture and shape into balls. Put them on the prepared cookie sheets spaced well apart and flatten slightly.

4. Bake for 12–15 minutes. Let cool on the cookie sheets for 5–10 minutes, then using a metal spatula, carefully transfer to wire racks to cool completely.

Makes about 30

* 1 cup butter, softened
* scant ¾ cup superfine sugar
* 1 egg yolk, lightly beaten
* 2 tsp vanilla extract
* 2¼ cups all-purpose flour
  ¼ cup unsweetened cocoa powder
  12 oz/350 g bittersweet chocolate, chopped
  ¼ cup dried sour cherries
* salt

2

Chocolate Fudge Squares

1. Put the butter and sugar into a bowl and mix well with a wooden spoon, then beat in the egg yolk and vanilla extract. Sift together the flour, unsweetened cocoa, and a pinch of salt into the mixture and stir until thoroughly combined. Halve the dough, shape into balls, wrap in plastic wrap, and chill in the refrigerator for 30–60 minutes.

2. Preheat the oven to 375°F/190°C. Line 2 cookie sheets with baking parchment.

3. Unwrap the dough and roll out between 2 sheets of baking parchment to about ⅛ inch/3 mm thick. Stamp out cookies with a 2½-inch/6-cm square cutter and put them on the prepared cookie sheets spaced well apart.

4. Bake for 10–15 minutes, until golden brown. Let cool on the cookie sheets for 5–10 minutes, then using a metal spatula, carefully transfer the cookies to wire racks to cool completely.

5. For the topping, put the fudge fingers into a heatproof bowl and melt over a saucepan of gently simmering water. Remove the bowl from the heat and gradually whisk in the cream. Let cool, then chill until spreadable. Spread the fudge topping over the cookies before serving.

Makes about 30

※ 1 cup butter, softened
※ scant ¾ cup golden superfine sugar
※ 1 egg yolk, lightly beaten
※ 2 tsp vanilla extract
※ 2 cups all-purpose flour
  ½ cup unsweetened cocoa powder
※ salt

Chocolate fudge topping
8 chocolate-coated fudge fingers, broken into pieces
4 tbsp heavy cream

Mega Chip Cookies

1. Preheat the oven to 375°F/190°C. Line 2–3 cookie sheets with baking parchment.

2. Put the butter and sugar into a bowl and mix well with a wooden spoon, then beat in the egg yolk and vanilla extract. Sift together the flour, unsweetened cocoa powder, and a pinch of salt into the mixture, add both kinds of chocolate chips, and stir until thoroughly combined.

3. Make 12 balls of the mixture, put them on the prepared cookie sheets, spaced well apart, and flatten slightly. Press the pieces of bittersweet chocolate into the cookies.

4. Bake for 12–15 minutes. Let cool on the cookie sheets for 5–10 minutes, then using a metal spatula, carefully transfer to wire racks to cool completely.

Makes 12 large cookies

- 1 cup butter, softened
- scant ¾ cup superfine sugar
- 1 egg yolk, lightly beaten
- 2 tsp vanilla extract
- 2 cups all-purpose flour
  - ½ cup unsweetened cocoa powder
  - ½ cup milk chocolate chips
  - ½ cup white chocolate chips
  - 4 oz/115 g bittersweet chocolate, coarsely chopped
- salt

Choco Mint Stars

1. Put the butter and sugar into a bowl and mix well with a wooden spoon, then beat in the egg yolk and peppermint extract. Sift together the flour and a pinch of salt into the mixture, add the coconut, and stir until thoroughly combined. Divide the mixture in half, shape into balls, and chill in the refrigerator for 30–60 minutes.

2. Preheat the oven to 375°F/190°C. Line 2 cookie sheets with baking parchment.

3. Unwrap the dough and roll out between 2 sheets of baking parchment to about ⅛ inch/3 mm thick and stamp out stars with a 2½–2¾-inch/6–7-cm cutter. Put them on the prepared cookie sheets spaced well apart.

4. Bake for 10–12 minutes, until light golden brown. Let cool on the cookie sheets for 5–10 minutes, then using a metal spatula, carefully transfer the cookies to wire racks to cool completely.

5. Melt the white chocolate and the milk chocolate in separate heatproof bowls set over a saucepan of gently simmering water. With the cooled cookies still on the racks, drizzle first with melted white chocolate and then with melted milk chocolate using a teaspoon. Let set.

Makes about 30

* 1 cup butter, softened
* scant ¾ cup superfine sugar
* 1 egg yolk, lightly beaten
  1 tsp peppermint extract
* 2½ cups all-purpose flour
  generous 1 cup unsweetened dried coconut
  3½ oz/100 g white chocolate, broken into pieces
  3½ oz/100 g milk chocolate, broken into pieces
* salt

5

Almond & Raspberry Jam Drops

1. Preheat the oven to 375°F/190°C. Line 2 cookie sheets with baking parchment.

2. Put the butter and sugar into a bowl and mix well with a wooden spoon, then beat in the egg yolk and almond extract. Sift together the flour and a pinch of salt into the mixture, add the almonds and candied peel, and stir until thoroughly combined.

3. Scoop out tablespoons of the mixture and shape on balls with your hands, then put them on the prepared cookie sheets spaced well apart. Use the dampened handle of a wooden spoon to make a hollow in the center of each cookie and fill the hollows with raspberry jam.

4. Bake for 12–15 minutes, until golden brown. Let cool on the cookie sheets for 5–10 minutes, then using a metal spatula, carefully transfer the cookies to wire racks to cool completely.

Makes about 25

* 1 cup butter, softened
* scant ¾ cup superfine sugar
* 1 egg yolk, lightly beaten
  2 tsp almond extract
* 2½ cups all-purpose flour
  ½ cup almonds, toasted and chopped
  ⅓ cup chopped candied peel
  4 tbsp raspberry jam
* salt

Orange & Chocolate Fingers

1. Put the butter, sugar, and orange rind into a bowl and mix well with a wooden spoon, then beat in the egg yolk and orange juice. Sift together the flour, ginger, and a pinch of salt into the mixture and stir until thoroughly combined. Shape the dough into a ball, wrap in plastic wrap, and chill in the refrigerator for 30–60 minutes.

2. Preheat the oven to 375°F/190°C. Line 2 cookie sheets with baking parchment.

3. Unwrap the dough and roll out between 2 sheets of baking parchment to a rectangle. Using a sharp knife, cut it into 4 x ¾-inch/10 x 2-cm strips and put them on the prepared cookie sheets spaced well apart.

4. Bake for 10–12 minutes, until light golden brown. Let cool on the cookie sheets for 5–10 minutes, then using a metal spatula, carefully transfer to wire racks to cool completely.

5. Put the pieces of chocolate into a heatproof bowl and melt over a saucepan of gently simmering water, then remove from the heat and let cool. When the chocolate is cool but not set, dip the cookies diagonally into it to half coat, then put on the wire racks and let set. You may find it easier to do this using tongs.

Makes about 35

* 1 cup butter, softened
* scant ¾ cup superfine sugar
  grated rind of 1 orange
* 1 egg yolk, lightly beaten
  2 tsp orange juice
* 2½ cups all-purpose flour
  1 tsp ground ginger
  4 oz/115 g bittersweet
  chocolate, broken into pieces
* salt

7

Traffic Lights

1. Put the butter and sugar into a bowl and mix well with a wooden spoon, then beat in the egg yolk and vanilla extract. Sift together the flour and a pinch of salt into the mixture, add the coconut, and stir until thoroughly combined. Halve the dough, roll each piece into a ball, wrap in plastic wrap, and chill in the refrigerator for 30–60 minutes.

2. Preheat the oven to 375°F/190°C. Line 2 cookie sheets with baking parchment.

3. Roll out each piece of dough between 2 sheets of baking parchment to a rectangle about ¼ inch/5 mm thick. Using a sharp knife, cut the dough into bars about 4 x ¾ inch/ 10 x 2 cm and put on the prepared cookie sheets spaced well apart.

4. Bake for 10–12 minutes, until golden brown. Let cool on the cookie sheets for 5–10 minutes, then using a metal spatula, carefully transfer the cookies to wire racks to cool completely.

5. To decorate, combine the egg white and lemon juice in a bowl, then gradually beat in the confectioners' sugar until smooth. With the cooled cookies still on the racks, spoon the frosting over them. Decorate some with a vertical row of red, yellow, and green candied cherries for traffic lights. Or if you prefer, use gelatin-based candies to make your own decorations. Let set.

Makes about 35–40

* 1 cup butter, softened
* scant ¾ cup superfine sugar
* 1 egg yolk, lightly beaten
* 2 tsp vanilla extract
* 2½ cups all-purpose flour, plus extra for dusting
  generous 1 cup unsweetened dried coconut
* salt

To decorate
1½ tbsp lightly beaten egg white
1½ tbsp lemon juice
1½ cups confectioners' sugar
red, yellow, and green candied cherries
gelatin-based candies (optional)

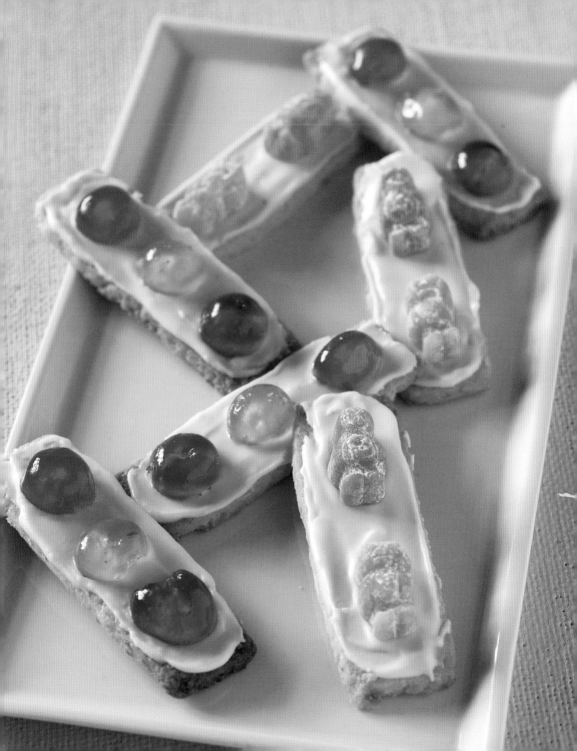

Sticky Ginger Cookies

1. Put the butter and sugar into a bowl and mix well with a wooden spoon, then beat in the egg yolk and ginger syrup. Sift together the flour and a pinch of salt into the mixture, add the preserved ginger and chocolate chips, and stir until thoroughly combined. Shape the mixture into a log, wrap in plastic wrap, and chill in the refrigerator for 30–60 minutes.

2. Preheat the oven to 375°F/190°C. Line 2 cookie sheets with baking parchment.

3. Unwrap the log and cut it into ¼-inch/5-mm slices with a sharp serrated knife. Put them on the prepared cookie sheets spaced well apart.

4. Bake for 12–15 minutes, until golden brown. Let cool on the cookie sheets for 5–10 minutes, then using a metal spatula, carefully transfer the cookies to wire racks to cool completely.

Makes 20

* 1 cup butter, softened
* scant ¾ cup golden superfine sugar
* 1 egg yolk, lightly beaten
  ¼ cup coarsely chopped preserved ginger, plus 1 tbsp syrup from the jar
* 2½ cups all-purpose flour
  ⅓ cup semisweet chocolate chips
* salt

Peanut Butter & Grape Jelly Cookies

1. Preheat the oven to 375°F/190°C. Line 2 cookie sheets with baking parchment.

2. Put the butter and sugar into a bowl and mix well with a wooden spoon, then beat in the egg yolk, vanilla extract, and peanut butter. Sift together the flour and a pinch of salt into the mixture and stir until thoroughly combined.

3. Scoop out tablespoons of the mixture and shape into balls with your hands, then put them on the prepared cookie sheets spaced well apart. Use the dampened handle of a wooden spoon to make a hollow in the center of each cookie and fill the hollows with grape jelly.

4. Bake for 12–15 minutes, until golden brown. Let cool on the cookie sheets for 5–10 minutes, then using a metal spatula, carefully transfer the cookies to wire racks to cool completely.

Makes about 25

* 1 cup butter, softened
* scant ¾ cup superfine sugar
* 1 egg yolk, lightly beaten
* 2 tsp vanilla extract
  scant ½ cup crunchy peanut butter
* 2½ cups all-purpose flour
  4 tbsp grape jelly
* salt

Caramel Glaze Cookies

1. Put the butter and sugar into a bowl and mix well with a wooden spoon, then beat in the egg yolk and vanilla extract. Sift together the flour and a pinch of salt into the mixture and stir until thoroughly combined. Halve the dough, shape into balls, wrap in plastic wrap, and chill in the refrigerator for 30–60 minutes.

2. To make the caramel glaze, have ready a bowl of cold water. Put the sugar and lemon juice into a saucepan and add 1½ tablespoons water. Heat gently, stirring constantly, until the sugar has dissolved, then boil, without stirring, until a rich caramel color. Remove the saucepan from the heat and plunge the bottom into the bowl of cold water. Stir in another 3 tablespoons of cold water and set the caramel aside to cool completely.

3. Line 2 cookie sheets with baking parchment. Unwrap the dough and roll out to about ⅛ inch/3 mm thick. Stamp out cookies with a 2½-inch/6-cm fluted cookie cutter and put them on the prepared cookie sheets.

4. Preheat the oven to 375°F/190°C. Beat the egg yolk with 1 tbsp of the caramel in a bowl and brush the glaze over the cookies. Let dry, then brush with the glaze again. Let dry, then brush the cookies with the glaze for a third time and make a pattern in it with a fork.

5. Bake the cookies for 10–12 minutes, until golden brown. Let cool on the cookie sheets for 5–10 minutes, then using a metal spatula, carefully transfer to wire racks to cool completely.

Makes about 30

* 1 cup butter, softened
* scant ¾ cup superfine sugar
* 1 egg yolk, lightly beaten
* 2 tsp vanilla extract
* 2½ cups all-purpose flour
* salt

Caramel glaze
¼ cup sugar
½ tsp lemon juice
1 egg yolk

Pear & Mint Cookies

1. Put the butter and sugar into a bowl and mix well with a wooden spoon, then beat in the egg yolk and vanilla extract. Sift together the flour and a pinch of salt into the mixture, add the pears, and stir until thoroughly combined. Shape the mixture into a log, wrap in plastic wrap, and chill in the refrigerator for 30–60 minutes.

2. Preheat the oven to 375°F/190°C. Line 2 cookie sheets with baking parchment.

3. Unwrap the log and cut it into ¼-inch/5-mm slices with a sharp serrated knife. Put them on the prepared cookie sheets spaced well apart.

4. Bake for 10–15 minutes, until golden brown. Let cool on the cookie sheets for 5–10 minutes, then using a metal spatula, carefully transfer the cookies to wire racks to cool completely.

5. To decorate, sift the confectioners' sugar into a bowl and stir in the peppermint extract. Gradually stir in the hot water until the frosting has the consistency of heavy cream. Stir in the food coloring. With the cooled cookies still on the wire racks, drizzle lines of frosting over them, using a teaspoon. Let set.

Makes about 30

* 1 cup butter, softened
* scant ¾ cup superfine sugar
* 1 egg yolk, lightly beaten
* 2 tsp vanilla extract
* 2½ cups all-purpose flour
  scant 1 cup finely chopped dried pears
* salt

To decorate
1 cup confectioners' sugar
few drops of peppermint extract
1 tbsp hot water
few drops of green food coloring

12

Chocolate, Date & Pecan Nut Pinwheels

1. Put the butter and scant ¾ cup of the sugar into a bowl and mix well with a wooden spoon, then beat in the egg yolk. Sift together the flour, unsweetened cocoa powder, and a pinch of salt into the mixture, add the pecan nuts, and stir until thoroughly combined. Halve the dough, shape into balls, wrap in plastic wrap, and chill for 30–60 minutes.

2. Meanwhile, put the dried dates, orange rind, orange flower water, and remaining sugar into a saucepan and cook over low heat, stirring constantly, until the sugar has dissolved. Bring to a boil, then lower the heat, and simmer, stirring occasionally, for 5 minutes. Remove the saucepan from the heat, pour the mixture into a bowl, and let cool, then chill in the refrigerator.

3. Unwrap the dough and roll out between 2 pieces of baking parchment to rectangles about 5 mm/¼ inch thick. Spread the date filling evenly over the rectangles. Roll up the dough from a short side like a jelly roll, wrap in the baking parchment, and chill for 30 minutes more.

4. Preheat the oven to 375°F/190°C. Line 2 cookie sheets with baking parchment.

5. Unwrap the rolls and cut into ½-inch/1-cm slices. Put them on the prepared cookie sheets and bake for 15–20 minutes, until golden brown. Let cool on the cookie sheets for 5–10 minutes, then using a metal spatula, carefully transfer the cookies to wire racks to cool completely.

Makes about 30

- ✴ 1 cup butter, softened
- ✴ 1 cup superfine sugar
- ✴ 1 egg yolk, lightly beaten
- ✴ 2 cups all-purpose flour
- ½ cup unsweetened cocoa powder
- scant 1 cup pecan nuts, finely ground
- 1⅔ cups coarsely chopped dried dates
- finely grated rind of 1 orange
- ¾ cup orange flower water
- ✴ salt

Cinnamon & Caramel Cookies

1. Preheat the oven to 375°F/190°C. Line 2 cookie sheets with baking parchment.

2. Put the butter and sugar into a bowl and mix well with a wooden spoon, then beat in the egg yolk and vanilla extract. Sift together the flour, cinnamon, allspice, and a pinch of salt into the mixture and stir until thoroughly combined.

3. Scoop up tablespoons of the mixture, shape into balls, and put on the prepared cookie sheets spaced well apart. Bake for 8 minutes. Place a caramel candy on top of each cookie, return to the oven, and bake for 6–7 minutes more.

4. Remove from the oven and let cool on the cookie sheets for 5–10 minutes. Using a metal spatula, carefully transfer the cookies to wire racks to cool completely.

Makes about 25

* 1 cup butter, softened
* scant ¾ cup superfine sugar
* 1 egg yolk, lightly beaten
* 1 tsp vanilla extract
* 2½ cups all-purpose flour
  1 tsp ground cinnamon
  ½ tsp allspice
  25–30 hard caramel candies
* salt

Marshmallow Daisies

1. Put the butter and sugar into a bowl and mix well with a wooden spoon, then beat in the egg yolk and vanilla extract. Sift together the flour, unsweetened cocoa powder, and a pinch of salt into the mixture and stir until thoroughly combined. Halve the dough, roll each piece into a ball, wrap in plastic wrap, and chill in the refrigerator for 30–60 minutes.

2. Preheat the oven to 375°F/190°C. Line 2 cookie sheets with baking parchment.

3. Unwrap the dough and roll out between 2 sheets of baking parchment to about ½ inch/1 cm thick and stamp out about 30 cookies with a 2-inch/5-cm flower cutter. Put them on the prepared cookie sheets spaced well apart.

4. Bake for 10–12 minutes, until firm. Remove the cookie sheets from the oven but do not turn off the heat. Arrange the pieces of marshmallow over the petals of the flowers, cutting them to fit if necessary. Return to the oven for 30–60 seconds, until the marshmallow has softened.

5. Let cool on the cookie sheets for 5–10 minutes, then using a metal spatula, carefully transfer the cookies to wire racks to cool completely. Meanwhile, heat the peach preserve in a small saucepan, strain into a bowl, and let cool. Pipe a small glob of peach preserve in the center of each flower and top with the sugar sprinkles.

Makes about 30

* 1 cup butter, softened
* scant ¾ cup superfine sugar
* 1 egg yolk, lightly beaten
* 2 tsp vanilla extract
* 2 cups all-purpose flour
  ½ cup unsweetened cocoa powder
  about 90 white mini marshmallows, halved horizontally
  4 tbsp peach preserve
  4 tbsp yellow sugar sprinkles
* salt

Peanut Partners

1. Put the butter and sugar into a bowl and mix well with a wooden spoon, then beat in the egg yolk. Sift together the flour, ginger, and a pinch of salt into the mixture, add the lemon rind, and stir until thoroughly combined. Halve the dough, shape into balls, wrap in plastic wrap, and chill in the refrigerator for 30–60 minutes.

2. Preheat the oven to 375°F/190°C. Line 2 cookie sheets with baking parchment.

3. Unwrap the dough and roll out between 2 sheets of baking parchment to about ⅛ inch/3 mm thick. Stamp out cookies with a 2½-inch/6-cm fluted cookie cutter and put them on the prepared cookie sheets spaced well apart.

4. Bake for 10–15 minutes, until golden brown. Let cool on the cookie sheets for 5–10 minutes, then using a metal spatula, carefully transfer the cookies to wire racks to cool completely.

5. Beat together the peanut butter and confectioners' sugar in a bowl, adding a little water if necessary. Spread the cookies with the peanut butter mixture and decorate with whole or chopped peanuts.

Makes about 30

* 1 cup butter, softened
* scant ¾ cup superfine sugar
* 1 egg yolk, lightly beaten
* 2½ cups all-purpose flour
  1 tsp ground ginger
  2 tsp finely grated lemon rind
  3 tbsp smooth peanut butter
  3 tbsp confectioners' sugar
* salt
  whole or chopped roasted
  peanuts, to decorate

Melt-in-the middles

1. Preheat the oven to 375°F/190°C. Line 2 cookie sheets with baking parchment.

2. For the filling, whisk the egg until soft peaks form, then gradually whisk in the sugar. Gently fold in the coconut, flour, and papaya. Set aside.

3. Melt the chocolate in a heatproof bowl set over a saucepan of barely simmering water, then remove from the heat. Put the butter and sugar into a bowl and mix well, then beat in the egg yolk and vanilla extract. Sift together the flour, unsweetened cocoa powder, and a pinch of salt into the mixture and stir until thoroughly combined. Stir in the melted chocolate and knead lightly.

4. Roll out the dough between 2 sheets of baking parchment to ¼–⅜ inch/5–8 mm thick. Stamp out cookies with a 2¾-inch/7-cm fluted round cutter and put them on the prepared cookie sheets. Using a 1¼-inch/3-cm plain round cutter, stamp out the centers and remove them. Bake for 8 minutes, then remove the cookie sheets from the oven and lower the temperature to 325°F/160°C. Spoon the middle mixture into the center of the cookies. Crumple 2 sheets of foil and place them over the cookie sheets but without their touching the cookies. Return to the oven and bake for 15–20 minutes more, until the middles are firm. Let cool on the cookie sheets for 5–10 minutes, then transfer to wire racks to cool completely.

Makes about 30

3 oz/85 g bittersweet chocolate broken into pieces

※ ½ cup butter, softened

※ scant ¾ cup golden superfine sugar

※ 1 egg yolk, lightly beaten

※ 2 tsp vanilla extract

※ 2½ cups all-purpose flour

1 tbsp unsweetened cocoa powder

※ salt

Filling

1 egg white

¼ cup superfine sugar

1 cup unsweetened dried coconut

1 tsp all-purpose flour

2 tbsp finely chopped plumped dried papaya

Chocolate Sprinkle Cookies

1. Put the butter and sugar into a bowl and mix well with a wooden spoon, then beat in the egg yolk and vanilla extract. Sift together the flour, unsweetened cocoa powder, and a pinch of salt into the mixture and stir until thoroughly combined. Halve the dough, roll each piece into a ball, wrap in plastic wrap, and chill in the refrigerator for 30–60 minutes.

2. Preheat the oven to 375°F/190°C. Line 2 cookie sheets with baking parchment.

3. Unwrap the dough and roll out between 2 pieces of baking parchment to about ¼ inch/5 mm thick and stamp out 30 cookies with a 2½–2¾-inch/6–7-cm fluted round cutter. Put them on the prepared cookie sheets spaced well apart.

4. Bake for 10–12 minutes. Let cool on the cookie sheets for 5–10 minutes, then using a metal spatula, carefully transfer the cookies to wire racks to cool completely.

5. Put the pieces of white chocolate into a heatproof bowl and melt over a saucepan of gently simmering water, then immediately remove from the heat. Spread the melted chocolate over the cookies, let cool slightly, and then sprinkle with the chocolate sprinkles. Let cool and set.

Makes about 30

* 1 cup butter, softened
* scant ¾ cup superfine sugar
* 1 egg yolk, lightly beaten
* 2 tsp vanilla extract
* 2 cups all-purpose flour, plus extra for dusting
  ½ cup unsweetened cocoa powder
  7 oz/200 g white chocolate, broken into pieces
  ⅓ cup chocolate sprinkles
* salt

18

Spicy Cinnamon Cookies

1. Put the butter, molasses, and sugar into a bowl and mix well with a wooden spoon, then beat in the egg yolk. Sift together the flour, cinnamon, nutmeg, cloves, and a pinch of salt into the mixture, add the walnuts, and stir until thoroughly combined. Halve the dough, shape into balls, wrap in plastic wrap, and chill in the refrigerator for 30–60 minutes.

2. Preheat the oven to 375°F/190°C. Line 2 cookie sheets with baking parchment.

3. Unwrap the dough and roll out between 2 sheets of baking parchment to about ¼ inch/5 mm thick. Stamp out cookies with a 2½-inch/6-cm fluted cutter and put them on the prepared cookie sheets.

4. Bake for 10–15 minutes, until firm. Let cool on the cookie sheets for 5–10 minutes, then using a metal spatula, carefully transfer the cookies to wire racks to cool completely.

5. To decorate, sift the confectioners' sugar into a bowl, then gradually stir in the hot water until the frosting has the consistency of thick cream. Spoon half the frosting into another bowl and stir a few drops of yellow food coloring into one bowl and a few drops of pink food coloring into the other. With the cookies still on the racks, using teaspoons, drizzle the yellow frosting over them in one direction and the pink icing over them at right angles. Let set.

Makes about 25

* scant 1 cup butter, softened
2 tbsp molasses
* scant ¾ cup superfine sugar
* 1 egg yolk, lightly beaten
* 2½ cups all-purpose flour
1 tsp ground cinnamon
½ tsp grated nutmeg
½ tsp ground cloves
2 tbsp chopped walnuts
* salt

To decorate
1 cup confectioners' sugar
1 tbsp hot water
a few drops of yellow food coloring
a few drops of pink food coloring

19

Chewy Candied Fruit Cookies

1. Put the butter and sugar into a bowl and mix well with a wooden spoon, then beat in the egg yolk and vanilla extract. Sift together the flour and a pinch of salt into the mixture and stir until thoroughly combined. Halve the dough, shape into balls, wrap in plastic wrap, and chill for 30–60 minutes.

2. Preheat the oven to 375°F/190°C. Line 2 cookie sheets with baking parchment.

3. Unwrap the dough and roll out between 2 sheets of baking parchment. Stamp out cookies with a 2½-inch/6-cm plain round cutter and put them on the prepared cookie sheets spaced well apart.

4. For the topping, put the syrup, butter, and sugar into a saucepan and melt over low heat, stirring occasionally. Meanwhile, put the fruit, candied peel, nuts, and flour into a bowl and mix well. When the syrup mixture is thoroughly combined, stir it into the fruit mixture. Divide the candied topping among the cookies, gently spreading it out to the edges.

5. Bake for 10–15 minutes, until firm. Let cool on the cookie sheets for 5–10 minutes, then using a metal spatula, carefully transfer the cookies to wire racks to cool completely.

Makes about 30

* 1 cup butter, softened
* scant ¾ cup superfine sugar
* 1 egg yolk, lightly beaten
* 2 tsp vanilla extract
* 2½ cups all-purpose flour
* salt

Candied topping
4 tbsp maple syrup
¼ cup butter
¼ cup superfine sugar
½ cup chopped plumped dried peaches
¼ cup candied cherries, chopped
⅓ cup chopped candied peel
¾ cup chopped macadamia nuts
¼ cup all-purpose flour

20

Chocolate Spread & Hazelnut Drops

1. Preheat the oven to 375°F/190°C. Line 2 cookie sheets with baking parchment.

2. Put the butter and sugar into a bowl and mix well with a wooden spoon, then beat in the egg yolk and vanilla extract. Sift together the flour, unsweetened cocoa, and a pinch of salt into the mixture, add the ground hazelnuts and chocolate chips, and stir until thoroughly combined.

3. Scoop out tablespoons of the mixture and shape into balls with your hands, then put them on the prepared cookie sheets spaced well apart. Use the dampened handle of a wooden spoon to make a hollow in the center of each cookie.

4. Bake for 12–15 minutes. Let cool on the cookie sheets for 5–10 minutes, then using a metal spatula, carefully transfer the cookies to wire racks to cool completely. When they have cooled down completely, fill the hollows in the center with chocolate and hazelnut spread.

Makes about 30

* 1 cup butter, softened
* scant ¾ cup superfine sugar
* 1 egg yolk, lightly beaten
* 2 tsp vanilla extract
* 2 cups all-purpose flour
  ½ cup unsweetened cocoa powder
  ½ cup ground hazelnuts
  ⅓ cup semisweet chocolate chips
  4 tbsp chocolate and hazelnut spread
* salt

Crunch

Chocolate Chip & Cinnamon Cookies

1. Preheat the oven to 375°F/190°C. Line 2 cookie sheets with baking parchment.

2. Put the butter and sugar into a bowl and mix well with a wooden spoon, then beat in the egg yolk and orange extract. Sift together the flour and a pinch of salt into the mixture, add the chocolate chips, and stir until thoroughly combined.

3. For the coating, mix together the sugar and cinnamon in a shallow dish. Scoop out tablespoons of the cookie dough, roll them into balls, then roll them in the cinnamon mixture to coat. Put them on the prepared cookie sheets spaced well apart.

4. Bake for 12–15 minutes. Let cool on the cookie sheets for 5–10 minutes, then using a metal spatula, carefully transfer to wire racks to cool completely.

Makes about 30

* 1 cup butter, softened
* scant ¾ cup superfine sugar
* 1 egg yolk, lightly beaten
  2 tsp orange extract
* 2½ cups all-purpose flour
  generous ½ cup semisweet chocolate chips
* salt

Cinnamon coating
1½ tbsp superfine sugar
1½ tbsp ground cinnamon

Almond Crunchies

1. Put the butter and sugar into a bowl and mix well with a wooden spoon, then beat in the egg yolk and almond extract. Sift together the flour and a pinch of salt into the mixture, add the almonds, and stir until thoroughly combined. Halve the dough, shape it into balls, wrap in plastic wrap, and chill in the refrigerator for 30–60 minutes.

2. Preheat the oven to 375°F/190°C. Line 2–3 cookie sheets with baking parchment.

3. Shape the dough into about 50 small balls and flatten them slightly between the palms of your hands. Put on the prepared cookie sheets spaced well apart.

4. Bake for 15–20 minutes, until golden brown. Let cool on the cookie sheets for 5–10 minutes, then using a metal spatula, carefully transfer to wire racks to cool completely.

Makes about 50

* 1 cup butter, softened
* scant ¾ cup superfine sugar
* 1 egg yolk, lightly beaten
  ½ tsp almond extract
* 2 cups all-purpose flour
  2 cups blanched almonds, chopped
* salt

23

Flower Gems

1. Put the butter and sugar into a bowl and mix well with a wooden spoon, then beat in the egg yolk and lemon juice. Sift together the flour and a pinch of salt into the mixture, add the tea leaves, and stir until thoroughly combined. Halve the dough, shape it into balls, wrap in plastic wrap, and chill in the refrigerator for 30–60 minutes.

2. Preheat the oven to 375°F/190°C. Line 2 cookie sheets with baking parchment.

3. Roll out the dough between 2 sheets of baking parchment to about ⅛ inch/3 mm thick. Stamp out flowers with a 2-inch/5-cm flower cutter. Put them on the prepared cookie sheets spaced well apart.

4. Bake for 10–12 minutes, until golden brown. Let cool on the cookie sheets for 5–10 minutes, then using a metal spatula, carefully transfer the cookies to wire racks to cool completely.

5. To decorate, mix the lemon juice with 1 tbsp water in a bowl, then gradually stir in enough confectioners' sugar to make a mixture with the consistency of thick cream. Divide the frosting among 4 separate bowls and add a drop of different food coloring to each.

6. With the cookies still on the racks, spread orange frosting on one-fourth of the cookies, pink on another fourth and so on. When the frosting is just beginning to set, put a matching sugar flower in the center of each cookie. Let set completely.

Makes about 30

* 1 cup butter, softened
* scant ¾ cup superfine sugar
* 1 egg yolk, lightly beaten
  1 tsp lemon juice
* 2½ cups all-purpose flour
  2 tbsp jasmine tea leaves
* salt

To decorate
1 tbsp lemon juice
1¾ cups confectioners' sugar
orange, pink, blue, and yellow food coloring
orange, pink, blue, and yellow sugar flowers

24

Snickerdoodles

1. Put the butter and sugar into a bowl and mix well with a wooden spoon, then beat in the eggs and vanilla extract. Sift together the flour, baking soda, nutmeg, and a pinch of salt into the mixture, add the pecan nuts, and stir until thoroughly combined. Shape the dough into a ball, wrap in plastic wrap, and chill in the refrigerator for 30–60 minutes.

2. Preheat the oven to 375°F/190°C. Line 2–3 cookie sheets with baking parchment.

3. For the coating, mix together the superfine sugar and cinnamon in a shallow dish. Scoop up tablespoons of the cookie dough and roll into balls. Roll each ball in the cinnamon mixture to coat and put on the prepared cookie sheets spaced well apart.

4. Bake for 10–12 minutes, until golden brown. Let cool on the cookie sheets for 5–10 minutes, then using a metal spatula, carefully transfer to wire racks to cool completely.

Makes about 40

* 1 cup butter, softened
* scant ¾ cup superfine sugar
* 2 extra large eggs, lightly beaten
* 1 tsp vanilla extract
* 3½ cups all-purpose flour
  1 tsp baking soda
  ½ tsp freshly grated nutmeg
  ½ cup finely chopped pecan nuts
* salt

Cinnamon coating
1 tbsp superfine sugar
2 tsp ground cinnamon

25

Lavender Cookies

1. Preheat the oven to 375°F/190°C. Line 2 cookie sheets with baking parchment.

2. Put the butter and sugar into a bowl and mix well with a wooden spoon, then beat in the egg. Sift together the flour and baking powder into the mixture, add the lavender, and stir until thoroughly combined.

3. Put tablespoons of the mixture on the prepared cookie sheets spaced well apart. Bake for 15 minutes, until golden brown. Let cool on the cookie sheets for 5–10 minutes, then using a metal spatula, carefully transfer to wire racks to cool completely.

Makes about 40

* 1 cup butter, softened
* generous ¾ cup superfine sugar
* 1 extra large egg, lightly beaten
* 2¼ cups all-purpose flour
  2 tsp baking powder
  1 tbsp dried lavender, chopped

Rose Flower Cookies

1. Put the butter and sugar into a bowl and mix well with a wooden spoon, then beat in the egg and rose water. Sift together the flour, baking powder, and a pinch of salt into the mixture and stir until thoroughly combined. Shape the dough into a log, wrap in plastic wrap, and chill in the refrigerator for 1–2 hours.

2. Preheat the oven to 375°F/190°C. Line 2–3 cookie sheets with baking parchment.

3. Unwrap the dough and cut into thin slices with a sharp serrated knife. Put on the prepared cookie sheets spaced well apart. Bake for 10–12 minutes, until light golden brown. Let the cookies cool on the cookie sheets for 10 minutes, then using a metal spatula, carefully transfer them to wire racks to cool completely.

4. To make the frosting, lightly beat the egg white with a fork in a bowl. Sift in half the confectioners' sugar and stir well, then sift in the remaining confectioners' sugar and flour, and mix in sufficient rose water to make a smooth, easy-to-spread frosting. Stir in a few drops of pink food coloring.

5. Let the cookies stand on the racks. Gently spread the frosting over them and let set.

Makes about 55–60

* 1 cup butter, softened
* generous 1 cup superfine sugar
* 1 extra large egg, lightly beaten
  1 tbsp rose water
* 2½ cups all-purpose flour
  1 tsp baking powder
* salt

Frosting
1 egg white
2¼ cups confectioners' sugar
2 tsp all-purpose flour
2 tsp rose water
pink food coloring

Alphabet Cookies

1. Put the butter and sugar into a bowl and mix well with a wooden spoon, then beat in the egg yolk and grenadine. Sift together the flour and a pinch of salt into the mixture and stir until thoroughly combined. Halve the dough, shape into balls, wrap in plastic wrap, and chill in the refrigerator for 30–60 minutes.

2. Preheat the oven to 375°F/190°C. Line 2 cookie sheets with baking parchment.

3. Unwrap the dough and roll out between 2 sheets of baking parchment to about ⅛ inch/3 mm thick. Sprinkle half the seeds over each piece of dough and lightly roll the rolling pin over them. Stamp out letters with alphabet cutters and put them on the prepared cookie sheets spaced well apart.

4. Bake for 10–12 minutes, until golden brown. Let cool on the cookie sheets for 5–10 minutes, then using a metal spatula, carefully transfer the cookies to wire racks to cool completely.

Makes about 30

* 1 cup butter, softened
* scant ¾ cup superfine sugar
* 1 egg yolk, lightly beaten
  2 tsp grenadine
* 2½ cups all-purpose flour
  5–6 tbsp dried pomegranate seeds or unsalted roasted melon seeds
* salt

Number Crunchers

1. Put the butter and sugar into a bowl and mix well with a wooden spoon, then beat in the egg yolk and vanilla extract. Sift together the flour, ginger, cinnamon, cloves, and a pinch of salt into the mixture and stir until thoroughly combined. Halve the dough, shape into balls, wrap in plastic wrap, and chill in the refrigerator for 30–60 minutes.

2. Preheat the oven to 375°F/190°C. Line 2 cookie sheets with baking parchment.

3. Unwrap the dough and roll out between 2 sheets of baking parchment to about ⅛ inch/3 mm thick. Sprinkle half the nuts over each piece of dough and lightly roll the rolling pin over them. Stamp out numbers with number-shaped cutters and put them on the prepared cookie sheets spaced well apart.

4. Bake for 10–12 minutes, until golden brown. Let cool on the cookie sheets for 5–10 minutes, then using a metal spatula, carefully transfer the cookies to wire racks to cool completely.

Makes about 35

* 1 cup butter, softened
* scant ¾ cup superfine sugar
* 1 egg yolk, lightly beaten
* 2 tsp vanilla extract
* 2½ cups all-purpose flour
  1 tsp ground ginger
  ¼ tsp ground cinnamon
  ¼ tsp ground cloves
  4–5 tbsp chopped macadamia nuts
* salt

Fennel & Angelica Cookies

1. Put the butter and sugar into a bowl and mix well with a wooden spoon, then beat in the egg yolk and angelica. Sift together the flour and a pinch of salt into the mixture, add the fennel seeds, and stir until thoroughly combined. Shape the dough into a log, wrap in plastic wrap, and chill in the refrigerator for 30–60 minutes.

2. Preheat the oven to 375°F/190°C. Line 2 cookie sheets with baking parchment.

3. Unwrap the dough and cut into ½-inch/1-cm slices with a sharp serrated knife. Put them on the prepared cookie sheets spaced well apart.

4. Bake for 12–15 minutes, until golden brown. Let cool on the cookie sheets for 5–10 minutes, then using a metal spatula, carefully transfer to wire racks to cool completely.

Makes about 20

* 1 cup butter, softened
* scant ¾ cup superfine sugar
* 1 egg yolk, lightly beaten
  1 tbsp finely chopped angelica
* 2½ cups all-purpose flour
  1 tablespoon fennel seeds
* salt

Cashew & Poppy Seed Cookies

1. Put the butter and sugar into a bowl and mix well with a wooden spoon, then beat in the egg yolk. Sift together the flour, cinnamon, and a pinch of salt into the mixture, add the nuts, and stir until thoroughly combined. Shape the dough into a log. Spread out the poppy seeds in a shallow dish and roll the log in them until well coated. Wrap in plastic wrap and chill in the refrigerator for 30–60 minutes.

2. Preheat the oven to 375°F/190°C. Line 2 cookie sheets with baking parchment.

3. Unwrap the dough and cut into ½-inch/1-cm slices with a sharp serrated knife. Put them on the prepared cookie sheets and bake for 12 minutes, until golden brown. Let cool on the cookie sheets for 5–10 minutes, then using a metal spatula, carefully transfer to wire racks to cool completely.

Makes about 20

* 1 cup butter, softened
* scant ¾ cup superfine sugar
* 1 egg yolk, lightly beaten
* 2½ cups all-purpose flour
  1 tsp ground cinnamon
  1 cup cashew nuts, chopped
  2–3 tbsp poppy seeds
* salt

Lemon & Sesame Seed Cookies

1. Dry-fry the sesame seeds in a heavy skillet over low heat, stirring frequently, for 2–3 minutes, until they give off their aroma. Remove the skillet from the heat and set aside to cool.

2. Put the butter, sugar, and toasted seeds into a bowl and mix well with a wooden spoon, then beat in the lemon rind and egg yolk. Sift together the flour and a pinch of salt into the mixture and stir until thoroughly combined. Halve the dough, form it into balls, wrap in plastic wrap, and chill in the refrigerator for 30–60 minutes.

3. Preheat the oven to 375°F/190°C. Line 2 cookie sheets with baking parchment. Unwrap the dough and roll out between 2 sheets of baking parchment. Stamp out cookies with a 2½-inch/6-cm round cutter and put them on the prepared cookie sheets spaced well apart.

4. Bake for 10–12 minutes, until light golden brown. Let cool on the cookie sheets for 5–10 minutes, then using a metal spatula, carefully transfer the cookies to wire racks to cool completely.

5. For the frosting, sift the confectioners' sugar into a bowl, add the lemon extract, and gradually stir in the hot water until the frosting is smooth and has the consistency of thick cream. Leave the cooled cookies on the racks and spread the frosting over them. Let set.

Makes about 30

2 tbsp sesame seeds
1 cup butter, softened
scant ¾ cup superfine sugar
1 tbsp finely grated lemon rind
1 egg yolk, lightly beaten
2½ cups all-purpose flour
salt

Frosting
1 cup confectioners' sugar
few drops of lemon extract
1 tbsp hot water

76

Walnut & Coffee Cookies

1. Put the instant latte into a bowl and stir in the hot, but not boiling water to make a paste. Put the butter and sugar into a bowl and mix well with a wooden spoon, then beat in the egg yolk and coffee paste. Sift together the flour and a pinch of salt into the mixture, add the walnuts, and stir until thoroughly combined. Halve the dough, shape into balls, wrap in plastic wrap, and chill in the refrigerator for 30–60 minutes.

2. Preheat the oven to 375°F/190°C. Line 2 cookie sheets with baking parchment.

3. Unwrap the dough and roll out between 2 sheets of baking parchment to about ⅛ inch/3 mm thick. Stamp out cookies with a 2½-inch/6-cm round cutter and put them on the prepared cookie sheets spaced well apart.

4. Lightly brush the cookies with water, sprinkle with the coffee sugar crystals, and bake for 10–12 minutes. Let cool on the cookie sheets for 5–10 minutes, then using a metal spatula, carefully transfer the cookies to wire racks to cool completely.

Makes about 30

2 envelopes instant latte

1 tbsp hot water

* 1 cup butter, softened

* scant ¾ cup superfine sugar

* 1 egg yolk, lightly beaten

* 2½ cups all-purpose flour

scant 1 cup finely chopped walnuts

* salt

coffee sugar crystals, for sprinkling

Neapolitan Cookies

1. Put the butter and sugar into a bowl and mix well with a wooden spoon, then beat in the egg yolk. Divide the mixture equally among 3 bowls.

2. Beat the vanilla extract into the first bowl. Sift together one-third of the flour and a pinch of salt into the mixture and stir until combined. Shape into a ball, wrap in plastic wrap, and chill in the refrigerator for 30–60 minutes. Sift together one-third of the flour, the unsweetened cocoa powder, and a pinch of salt into the second bowl and stir until thoroughly combined. Shape into a ball, wrap in plastic wrap, and chill in the refrigerator. Beat the almond extract into the third bowl. Sift together the remaining flour and a pinch of salt and stir until thoroughly combined. Mix in a few drops of green food coloring, then form into a ball, wrap in plastic wrap, and chill in the refrigerator.

3. Preheat the oven to 375°F/190°C. Line 2 cookie sheets with baking parchment. Roll out each piece of dough between 2 sheets of baking parchment to rectangles the same size. Brush the top of the vanilla dough with a little egg white and place the chocolate rectangle on top. Brush with a little beaten egg white and place the almond rectangle on top. Using a sharp knife, cut into ¼-inch/5-mm thick slices, then cut each slice in half.

4. Put on the prepared cookie sheets and bake for 10–12 minutes. Let cool for 5-10 minutes, then carefully transfer the cookies to wire racks to cool.

Makes about 20

* 1 cup butter, softened
* scant ¾ cup superfine sugar
* 1 egg yolk, lightly beaten
* 1 tsp vanilla extract
* 2½ cups all-purpose flour
  1 tbsp unsweetened cocoa powder
  ½ tsp almond extract
  few drops of green food coloring
  1 egg white, lightly beaten
* salt

Biscotti

1. Put the butter, sugar, and lemon rind into a bowl and mix well with a wooden spoon, then beat in the egg yolk and brandy. Sift the flour and a pinch of salt into the mixture, add the pistachios, and stir until thoroughly combined. Shape the mixture into a log, flatten slightly, wrap in plastic wrap, and chill in the refrigerator for 30–60 minutes.

2. Preheat the oven to 375°F/190°C. Line 2 cookie sheets with baking parchment.

3. Unwrap the log and cut it slightly on the diagonal into ¼-inch/5-mm slices with a sharp serrated knife. Put them on the prepared cookie sheets spaced well apart.

4. Bake for 10 minutes, until golden brown. Using a metal spatula, carefully transfer the cookies to wire racks. Dust with confectioners' sugar and let cool.

Makes about 30

* 1 cup butter, softened
* scant ¾ cup superfine sugar
  finely grated rind of 1 lemon
* 1 egg yolk, lightly beaten
  2 tsp brandy
* 2½ cups all-purpose flour
  ¾ cup pistachios
* salt
  confectioners' sugar, for dusting

Golden Hazelnut Cookies

1. Put the butter and sugar into a bowl and mix well with a wooden spoon, then beat in the egg yolk. Sift together the flour and a pinch of salt into the mixture, add the ground hazelnuts, and stir until thoroughly combined. Halve the dough, form into balls, wrap in plastic wrap, and chill in the refrigerator for 30–60 minutes.

2. Preheat the oven to 375°F/190°C. Line 2 cookie sheets with baking parchment.

3. Unwrap the dough and roll out between 2 sheets of baking parchment. Stamp out cookies with a plain 2½-inch/6-cm cutter and put them on the prepared cookie sheets spaced well apart.

4. Bake for 10–12 minutes, until golden brown. Let cool on the cookie sheets for 5–10 minutes, then using a metal spatula, carefully transfer the cookies to wire racks to cool completely.

5. When the cookies are cool, place the wire racks over a sheet of baking parchment. Put the chocolate into a heatproof bowl and melt over a saucepan of gently simmering water. Remove the bowl from the heat and let cool, then spoon the chocolate over the cookies. Gently tap the wire racks to level the surface and let set.

6. Add a hazelnut to the center of each cookie and let set.

Makes about 30

* 1 cup butter, softened
* scant ¾ cup golden superfine sugar
* 1 egg yolk, lightly beaten
* 2 cups all-purpose flour
  ½ cup ground hazelnuts
* salt

To decorate
8 oz/225 g semisweet chocolate, broken into pieces
about 30 hazelnuts

36

Apricot & Pecan Cookies

① Put the butter and sugar into a bowl and mix well with a wooden spoon, then beat in the egg yolk and vanilla extract. Sift together the flour and a pinch of salt into the mixture, add the orange rind and apricots, and stir until thoroughly combined. Shape the dough into a log. Spread out the pecans in a shallow dish. Roll the log in the nuts until well coated, then wrap in plastic wrap, and chill in the refrigerator for 30–60 minutes.

② Preheat the oven to 375°F/190°C. Line 2 cookie sheets with baking parchment.

③ Unwrap the dough and cut into ¼-inch/5-mm slices with a sharp serrated knife. Put the slices on the prepared cookie sheets spaced well apart.

④ Bake for 10–12 minutes. Let cool on the cookie sheets for 5–10 minutes, then using a metal spatula, carefully transfer to wire racks to cool completely.

Makes about 30

* 1 cup butter, softened
* scant ¾ cup superfine sugar
* 1 egg yolk, lightly beaten
* 2 tsp vanilla extract
* 2½ cups all-purpose flour
  grated rind of 1 orange
  ¼ cup plumped dried apricots, chopped
  scant 1 cup finely chopped pecan nuts
* salt

37

Pistachio & Almond Cookies

1. Put the butter and sugar into a bowl and mix well with a wooden spoon, then beat in the egg yolk and almond extract. Sift together the flour and a pinch of salt into the mixture, add the ground almonds, and stir until thoroughly combined. Halve the dough, shape into balls, wrap in plastic wrap, and chill in the refrigerator for 30–60 minutes.

2. Preheat the oven to 375°F/190°C. Line 2 cookie sheets with baking parchment.

3. Unwrap the dough and roll out between 2 sheets of baking parchment to about ⅛ inch/3 mm thick. Sprinkle half the pistachios over each piece of dough and roll lightly with the rolling pin. Stamp out cookies with a heart-shaped cutter and put on the prepared cookie sheets spaced well apart.

4. Bake for 10–12 minutes. Let cool on the cookie sheets for 5–10 minutes, then using a metal spatula, carefully transfer the cookies to wire racks to cool completely.

Makes about 30

* 1 cup butter, softened
* scant ¾ cup superfine sugar
* 1 egg yolk, lightly beaten
2 tsp almond extract
* 2 cups all-purpose flour
½ cup ground almonds
½ cup finely chopped pistachios
* salt

Cappuccino Cookies

1. Empty the cappuccino sachets into a small bowl and stir in the hot, but not boiling water to make a paste.

2. Put the butter and sugar into a bowl and mix well with a wooden spoon, then beat in the egg yolk and cappuccino paste. Sift together the flour and a pinch of salt into the mixture and stir until thoroughly combined. Halve the dough, shape into balls, wrap in plastic wrap, and chill in the refrigerator for 30–60 minutes.

3. Preheat the oven to 375°F/190°C. Line 2 cookie sheets with baking parchment.

4. Unwrap the dough and roll out between 2 sheets of baking parchment. Stamp out cookies with a 2½-inch/6-cm plain cutter and put them on the prepared cookie sheets spaced well apart.

5. Bake for 10–12 minutes, until golden brown. Let cool on the cookie sheets for 5–10 minutes, then using a metal spatula, carefully transfer to wire racks to cool completely.

6. When the cookies are cool, place the wire racks over a sheet of baking parchment. Put the chocolate into a heatproof bowl and melt over a saucepan of gently simmering water. Remove the bowl from the heat and let cool, then spoon the chocolate over the cookies. Gently tap the wire racks to level the surface and let set. Scrape up the spilt chocolate from the baking parchment and return it to the bowl. Dust with cocoa powder.

Makes about 30

2 envelopes instant cappuccino
1 tbsp hot water
* 1 cup butter, softened
* scant ¾ cup superfine sugar
* 1 egg yolk, lightly beaten
* 2½ cups all-purpose flour
6 oz/175 g white chocolate, broken into pieces
* salt
unsweetened cocoa powder, for dusting

Chamomile Cookies

1. Put the butter and sugar into a bowl and mix well with a wooden spoon. If necessary, remove the tea leaves from the tea bags. Stir the tea into the butter mixture, then beat in the egg yolk and vanilla. Sift together the flour and a pinch of salt into the mixture and stir until thoroughly combined.

2. Shape the dough into a log. Spread out 3–4 tablespoons of superfine sugar in a shallow dish and roll the log in the sugar to coat. Wrap in plastic wrap and chill for 30–60 minutes.

3. Preheat the oven to 375°F/190°C. Line 2 cookie sheets with baking parchment.

4. Unwrap the log and cut into ¼-inch/5-mm slices with a sharp serrated knife. Put them on the prepared cookie sheets spread well apart.

5. Bake for about 10 minutes, until golden. Let cool on the cookie sheets for 5–10 minutes, then using a metal spatula, carefully transfer to wire racks to cool completely.

Makes about 30

* 1 cup butter, softened
* scant ¾ cup golden superfine sugar, plus extra for coating
* 1 tbsp (3–4 tea bags) chamomile or chamomile and lime flower infusion or tea leaves
* 1 egg yolk, lightly beaten
* 1 tsp vanilla extract
* 2½ cups all-purpose flour
* salt

40

Cinnamon & Orange Crisps

1. Put the butter, scant ¾ cup of the sugar, and the orange rind into a bowl and mix well with a wooden spoon, then beat in the egg yolk and 2 tsp of the orange juice. Sift together the flour and a pinch of salt into the mixture and stir until thoroughly combined. Shape the dough into a ball, wrap in plastic wrap, and chill for 30–60 minutes.

2. Unwrap the dough and roll out between 2 sheets of baking parchment into a 12-inch/30-cm square. Brush with the remaining orange juice and sprinkle with the cinnamon. Lightly roll with the rolling pin. Roll up the dough like a jelly roll. Wrap in plastic wrap and chill in the refrigerator for 30 minutes.

3. Preheat the oven to 375°F/190°C. Line 2 cookie sheets with baking parchment.

4. Unwrap the dough and using a sharp knife, cut into thin slices. Put them on the prepared cookie sheets spaced well apart and bake for 10–12 minutes. Let cool on the cookie sheets for 5–10 minutes, then using a metal spatula, carefully transfer to wire racks to cool completely.

Makes about 30

* 1 cup butter, softened
* 1 cup superfine sugar
  grated rind of 1 orange
* 1 egg yolk, lightly beaten
  4 tsp orange juice
* 2½ cups all-purpose flour
  2 tsp ground cinnamon
* salt

Party

41

Chocolate & Ginger Checkerboard Cookies

1. Put the butter and sugar into a bowl and mix well with a wooden spoon, then beat in the egg yolk and vanilla extract. Sift together the flour and a pinch of salt into the mixture and stir until thoroughly combined.

2. Divide the dough in half. Add the ginger and orange rind to one half and mix well. Shape the dough into a log 6 inches/ 15 cm long. Flatten the sides and top to square off the log to 2 inches/5 cm high. Wrap in plastic wrap and chill in the refrigerator for 30–60 minutes. Add the cocoa to the other half of the dough and mix well. Shape into a flattened log exactly the same size as the first one, wrap in plastic wrap, and chill in the refrigerator for 30–60 minutes.

3. Unwrap the dough and cut each flattened log lengthwise into 3 slices. Cut each slice lengthwise into 3 strips. Brush the strips with egg white and stack them in threes, alternating the flavors, to make the original flattened log shapes again. Wrap in plastic wrap and chill in the refrigerator for 30–60 minutes.

4. Preheat the oven to 375°F/190°C. Line 2 cookie sheets with baking parchment.

5. Unwrap the logs and cut into slices with a sharp serrated knife. Put the cookies on the prepared cookie sheets spaced well apart. Bake for 12–15 minutes, until firm. Let cool on the cookie sheets for 5–10 minutes, then using a metal spatula, carefully transfer to wire racks to cool completely.

Makes about 30

* 1 cup butter, softened
* scant ¾ cup superfine sugar
* 1 egg yolk, lightly beaten
* 2 tsp vanilla extract
* 2½ cups all-purpose flour
  1 tsp ground ginger
  1 tbsp finely grated orange rind
  1 tbsp unsweetened cocoa powder, sifted
  1 egg white, lightly beaten
* salt

42

Iced Stars

1. Put the butter and sugar into a bowl and mix well with a wooden spoon, then beat in the egg yolk and vanilla extract. Sift together the flour and a pinch of salt into the mixture and stir until thoroughly combined. Halve the dough, shape into balls, wrap in plastic wrap, and chill in the refrigerator for 30–60 minutes.

2. Preheat the oven to 375°F/190°C. Line 2 cookie sheets with baking parchment.

3. Unwrap the dough and roll out between 2 sheets of baking parchment to about ⅛ inch/3 mm thick. Stamp out cookies with a star-shaped cutter and put them on the prepared cookie sheets spaced well apart.

4. Bake for 10–15 minutes, until light golden brown. Let cool on the cookie sheets for 5–10 minutes, then using a metal spatula, carefully transfer to wire racks to cool completely.

5. To decorate, sift the confectioners' sugar into a bowl and stir in 1–2 tablespoons warm water until the mixture has the consistency of thick cream. Divide the frosting among 3–4 bowls and add a few drops of your chosen food colorings to each. With the cookies still on the racks, spread the different colored frostings over them to the edges. Arrange silver and gold balls on top and/or sprinkle with colored sprinkles or other decorations. If you prefer, color unsweetened dried coconut, shredded or flaked, with edible food coloring in a contrasting color. Let the cookies set.

Makes about 30

* 1 cup butter, softened
* scant ¾ cup superfine sugar
* 1 egg yolk, lightly beaten
* ½ tsp vanilla extract
* 2½ cups all-purpose flour
* salt

To decorate
1¾ cups confectioners' sugar
1–2 tbsp warm water
edible food colorings
silver and gold balls
colored sprinkles
unsweetened dried coconut
sugar sprinkles
sugar stars, hearts, and flowers

Chocolate Buttons

1. Empty the chocolate drink envelopes into a bowl and stir in the hot water to make a paste. Put the butter and sugar into a bowl and mix well with a wooden spoon, then beat in the egg yolk and chocolate paste. Sift together the flour and a pinch of salt into the mixture and stir until thoroughly combined. Halve the dough, shape into rounds, wrap in plastic wrap, and chill in the refrigerator for 30–60 minutes.

2. Preheat the oven to 375°F/190°C. Line 2 cookie sheets with baking parchment.

3. Unwrap the dough and roll out between 2 sheets of baking parchment to ⅛ inch/3 mm thick. Stamp out cookies with a plain 2-inch/5-cm cutter. Using a 1¼-inch/3-cm cap from a soda or mineral water bottle, make an indentation in the center of each button. Using a wooden toothpick, make 4 holes in the center of each button, then put them on the prepared cookie sheets spaced well apart. Sprinkle with superfine sugar.

4. Bake for 10–15 minutes, until firm. Let cool on the cookie sheets for 5–10 minutes, then using a metal spatula, transfer to wire racks to cool completely.

Makes about 30

2 envelopes instant chocolate or fudge chocolate drink
1 tbsp hot water
✳ 1 cup butter, softened
✳ scant ¾ cup superfine sugar, plus extra for sprinkling
✳ 1 egg yolk, lightly beaten
✳ 2½ cups all-purpose flour
✳ salt

Name Cookies

1. Put the butter and sugar into a bowl and mix well with a wooden spoon, then beat in the egg yolk, orange juice or liqueur, and grated rind. Sift together the flour and a pinch of salt into the mixture and stir until thoroughly combined. Halve the dough, shape into balls, wrap in plastic wrap, and chill in the refrigerator for 30–60 minutes.

2. Preheat the oven to 375°F/190°C. Line 2 cookie sheets with baking parchment.

3. Unwrap the dough and roll out to about ⅛ inch/3 mm thick. Depending on the occasion and age group, stamp out appropriate shapes with cookie cutters. Put the cookies on the prepared cookie sheets spaced well apart.

4. Bake for 10–15 minutes, until light golden brown. Let cool on the cookie sheets for 5–10 minutes, then transfer to wire racks to cool completely.

5. Leave the cookies on the racks. Put the egg white and confectioners' sugar into a bowl and beat until smooth, adding a very little water if necessary (the frosting should just hold its shape). Transfer half the frosting to another bowl and color each bowl of frosting with a different color. Put both frostings in pastry bags with fine tips or into small plastic bags (see page 7). Decorate as desired and add candies, green balls, or candied flowers. Let set.

Makes 25–30

* 1 cup butter, softened
* scant ¾ cup superfine sugar
* 1 egg yolk, lightly beaten
2 tsp orange juice or orange liqueur
grated rind of 1 orange
* 2½ cups all-purpose flour
* salt

To decorate
1 egg white
1 cup confectioners' sugar
few drops each of 2 edible food colors
small candies, green balls, or candied flowers

45

Turkish Delight Cookies

1. Put the butter and sugar into a bowl and mix well with a wooden spoon, then beat in the egg yolk and almond extract. Sift together the flour and a pinch of salt into the mixture, add the pistachios, and stir until thoroughly combined. Halve the dough, shape into balls, wrap in plastic wrap, and chill for 30–60 minutes.

2. Preheat the oven to 375°F/190°C. Line 2 cookie sheets with baking parchment.

3. Unwrap the dough and roll out between 2 sheets of baking parchment. Stamp out 2½-inch/6-cm squares and put them on the prepared cookie sheets.

4. Bake for 12–15 minutes, until light golden brown, then remove from the oven. Cover the tops of the cookies with halved mini marshmallows. Brush with water and sprinkle with the coconut. Return to the oven for about 30 seconds, until the marshmallows have softened. Let cool on the cookie sheets for 5–10 minutes, then using a metal spatula, transfer the cookies to wire racks to cool completely.

Makes about 30

* 1 cup butter, softened

scant ¾ cup rose petal-flavored superfine sugar (see page 8)

* 1 egg yolk, lightly beaten

1 tsp almond extract

* 2½ cups all-purpose flour

scant 1 cup chopped pistachios

1½ cups pink mini marshmallows, halved horizontally

⅓–⅔ cup unsweetened dried coconut

* salt

106

46

Sugared Hearts

1. Put the butter and half the sugar into a bowl and mix well with a wooden spoon, then beat in the egg yolk and vanilla extract. Sift together the flour, unsweetened cocoa powder, and a pinch of salt into the mixture and stir until thoroughly combined. Halve the dough, shape into balls, wrap in plastic wrap, and chill in the refrigerator for 30–60 minutes.

2. Preheat the oven to 375°F/190°C. Line 2 cookie sheets with baking parchment.

3. Unwrap the dough and roll out between 2 sheets of baking parchment. Stamp out cookies with a heart-shaped cutter and put them on the prepared cookie sheets spaced well apart.

4. Bake for 10–15 minutes, until firm. Let cool on the cookie sheets for 5–10 minutes, then using a metal spatula, carefully transfer to wire racks to cool completely.

5. Meanwhile, divide the remaining sugar among 4 small plastic bags or bowls. Add a little food coloring paste to each and rub in until well mixed. (Wear a plastic glove if mixing in bowls to prevent staining.) Put the chocolate in a heatproof bowl and melt over a saucepan of gently simmering water. Remove from the heat and let cool slightly.

6. Leave the cookies on the racks. Spread the melted chocolate over them and sprinkle with the colored sugar. Let set.

Makes about 30

- 1 cup butter, softened
- scant 1½ cups superfine sugar
- 1 egg yolk, lightly beaten
- 2 tsp vanilla extract
- 2¼ cups all-purpose flour
- ¼ cup unsweetened cocoa powder
- 3–4 food coloring pastes
- 3½ oz/100 g semisweet chocolate, broken into pieces
- salt

47

Chocolate Dominoes

1. Put the butter and sugar into a bowl and mix well with a wooden spoon, then beat in the egg yolk and vanilla extract. Sift together the flour, unsweetened cocoa powder, and a pinch of salt into the mixture, add the coconut, and stir until thoroughly combined. Halve the dough, shape into balls, wrap in plastic wrap, and chill in the refrigerator for 30–60 minutes.

2. Preheat the oven to 375°F/190°C. Line 2 cookie sheets with baking parchment.

3. Unwrap the dough and roll out between 2 sheets of baking parchment. Stamp out cookies with a 3½-inch/9-cm plain square cutter, then cut them in half to make rectangles. Put them on the prepared cookie sheets and using a knife, make a line across the center of each without cutting through. Arrange the chocolate chips on top of the cookies to look like dominoes, pressing them in gently.

4. Bake for 10–15 minutes, until golden brown. Let cool on the cookie sheets for 5–10 minutes, then using a metal spatula, carefully transfer to wire racks to cool completely.

Makes 28

* 1 cup butter, softened
* scant ¾ cup superfine sugar
* 1 egg yolk, lightly beaten
* 2 tsp vanilla extract
* 2¼ cups all-purpose flour
  ¼ cup unsweetened cocoa powder
  ⅓ cup unsweetened dried coconut
  scant ⅓ cup white chocolate chips
* salt

48

Butterfly Cookies

1. Put the malted drink in a bowl and stir in the hot, but not boiling water to make a paste.

2. Put the butter and sugar into a bowl and mix well with a wooden spoon, then beat in the egg yolk and malted drink paste. Sift together the flour and a pinch of salt into the mixture and stir until thoroughly combined. Halve the dough, shape into balls, wrap in plastic wrap, and chill in the refrigerator for 30–60 minutes. Preheat the oven to 375°F/190°C. Line 2 cookie sheets with baking parchment.

3. Unwrap the dough and roll out between 2 sheets of baking parchment. Stamp out cookies with a butterfly cutter and put them on the prepared cookie sheets.

4. Whisk an egg yolk and put a little of it in an egg cup. Add a few drops of food coloring and mix well. Using a fine paintbrush, paint a pattern on the butterflies' wings. Mix other colors with beaten egg yolk in egg cups and add to the pattern.

5. Bake for 10–15 minutes, until firm. Let cool on the cookie sheets for 5–10 minutes, then using a metal spatula, carefully transfer to wire racks to cool completely.

Makes about 20

2 envelopes instant malted food drink

1 tbsp hot water

* 1 cup butter, softened
* scant ¾ cup superfine sugar
* 1 egg yolk, lightly beaten
* 2½ cups all-purpose flour
* salt

To decorate
egg yolks
edible food coloring

49

Margarita Cookies

1. Preheat the oven to 375°F/190°C. Line 2 cookie sheets with baking parchment.

2. Put the butter, sugar, and lime rind into a bowl and mix well with a wooden spoon, then beat in the egg yolk and orange liqueur or orange extract. Sift together the flour and a pinch of salt into the mixture and stir until thoroughly combined.

3. Scoop up tablespoons of the dough and put them on the prepared cookie sheets, then flatten gently. Bake for 10–15 minutes, until light golden brown. Let cool on the cookie sheets for 5–10 minutes, then using a metal spatula, carefully transfer to wire racks to cool completely.

4. Sift the confectioners' sugar into a bowl and stir in sufficient tequila to give the mixture the consistency of thick cream. With the cookies still on the racks, drizzle the frosting over them with a teaspoon. Let set.

Makes about 30

* 1 cup butter, softened
* scant ¾ cup superfine sugar
  finely grated rind of 1 lime
* 1 egg yolk, lightly beaten
  2 tsp orange liqueur or 1 tsp orange extract
* 2½ cups all-purpose flour
* salt

To decorate
1¼ cups confectioners' sugar
2 tbsp white tequila

50

Peach Daiquiri Cookies

1. Preheat the oven to 375°F/190°C. Line 2 cookie sheets with baking parchment.

2. Put the butter, sugar, and lime rind into a bowl and mix well with a wooden spoon, then beat in the egg yolk, white rum, and dried peach. Sift together the flour and a pinch of salt into the mixture and stir until thoroughly combined.

3. Scoop up tablespoons of the dough and put them on the prepared cookie sheets, then flatten gently. Bake for 10–15 minutes, until light golden brown. Let cool on the cookie sheets for 5–10 minutes, then using a metal spatula, carefully transfer to wire racks to cool completely.

4. Sift the confectioners' sugar into a bowl and stir in sufficient white rum to give the mixture the consistency of thick cream. With the cookies still on the racks, drizzle the frosting over them with a teaspoon. Let set.

Makes about 30

* 1 cup butter, softened
* scant ¾ cup superfine sugar
  finely grated rind of 1 lime
* 1 egg yolk, lightly beaten
  2 tsp white rum
  scant 1 cup chopped
    plumped dried peach
* 2½ cups all-purpose flour
* salt

To decorate
1¼ cups confectioners' sugar
2 tbsp white rum

51

Classic Saffron Cookies

① Put the currants in a bowl, pour in the wine, and let soak for 1 hour. Drain the currants and reserve any remaining wine.

② Preheat the oven to 375°F/190°C. Line 2 cookie sheets with baking parchment.

③ Put the butter and sugar into a bowl and mix well with a wooden spoon, then beat in the egg yolk and 2 tsp of the reserved wine. Sift together the flour, saffron, and a pinch of salt into the mixture and stir until thoroughly combined.

④ Scoop up tablespoons of the dough and put them on the prepared cookie sheets spaced well apart. Flatten gently and smooth the tops with the back of the spoon.

⑤ Bake for 10–15 minutes, until light golden brown. Let cool on the cookie sheets for 5–10 minutes, then using a metal spatula, carefully transfer to wire racks to cool completely.

Makes about 30

scant ½ cup currants
½ cup sweet white wine
✳ 1 cup butter, softened
✳ scant ¾ cup superfine sugar
✳ 1 egg yolk, lightly beaten
✳ 2½ cups all-purpose flour
½ tsp powdered saffron
✳ salt

52

Caribbean Cookies

1. Preheat the oven to 375°F/190°C. Line 2 cookie sheets with baking parchment.

2. Put the butter and sugar into a bowl and mix well with a wooden spoon, then beat in the egg yolk and rum or rum flavoring. Sift together the flour and a pinch of salt into the mixture, add the coconut, and stir until thoroughly combined.

3. Scoop up tablespoons of the dough and put them on the prepared cookie sheets spaced well apart. Make a hollow in the center of each with the dampened handle of a wooden spoon. Fill the hollows with lime marmalade.

4. Bake for 10–15 minutes, until light golden brown. Let cool on the cookie sheets for 5–10 minutes, then using a metal spatula, carefully transfer to wire racks to cool completely.

Makes about 30

* 1 cup butter, softened
* scant ¾ cup superfine sugar
* 1 egg yolk, lightly beaten
   2 tsp rum or rum flavoring
* 2½ cups all-purpose flour
   generous 1 cup unsweetened
      dried coconut
   4 tbsp lime marmalade
* salt

53

Thanksgiving Cookies

1. Preheat the oven to 375°F/190°C. Line 2 cookie sheets with baking parchment.

2. Put the butter and sugar into a bowl and mix well with a wooden spoon, then beat in the egg yolk and orange juice. Sift together the flour and a pinch of salt into the mixture, add the blueberries, cranberries, and chocolate chips, and stir until thoroughly combined. Scoop up tablespoons of the dough and put them on the prepared cookie sheets spaced well apart.

3. Bake for 10–15 minutes, until light golden brown. Let cool on the cookie sheets for 5–10 minutes, then using a metal spatula, carefully transfer to wire racks to cool completely.

Makes about 30

* 1 cup butter, softened
* scant ¾ cup golden superfine sugar
* 1 egg yolk, lightly beaten
  2 tsp orange juice
* 2½ cups all-purpose flour
  ⅓ cup dried blueberries
  ½ cup fresh cranberries
  3 tbsp white chocolate chips
* salt

54

Double Heart Cookies

1. Put the instant latte into a small bowl and stir in the hot, but not boiling water to make a paste.

2. Put the butter and sugar into a bowl and mix well with a wooden spoon, then beat in the egg yolk. Divide the mixture in half. Beat the latte paste into one half. Sift 1¼ cups of the flour with a pinch of salt into the mixture and stir until thoroughly combined. Shape the dough into a ball, wrap in plastic wrap, and chill in the refrigerator for 30–60 minutes.

3. Beat the vanilla extract into the other bowl, then sift together the remaining flour, the unsweetened cocoa powder, and a pinch of salt into the mixture. Stir until thoroughly combined. Shape the dough into a ball, wrap in plastic wrap, and chill in the refrigerator for 30–60 minutes.

4. Preheat the oven to 375°F/190°C. Line 2 cookie sheets with baking parchment.

5. Unwrap both flavors of dough and roll out each between 2 sheets of baking parchment. Stamp out cookies with a 2¾-inch/7-cm heart-shaped cutter and put them on the prepared cookie sheets spaced well apart. Using a 1½–2-inch/4–5-cm heart-shaped cutter, stamp out the centers of each larger heart and remove from the cookie sheets. Put a small chocolate-flavored heart in the center of each large coffee-flavored heart and vice versa. Bake for 10–15 minutes. Let cool for 5-10 minutes, then transfer to wire racks to cool completely.

Makes about 30

1 envelope instant latte
1½ tsp hot water
1 cup butter, softened
scant ¾ cup superfine sugar
1 egg yolk, lightly beaten
2¼ cups all-purpose flour
1 tsp vanilla extract
3 tbsp unsweetened cocoa powder
salt

Easter Nest Cookies

1. Put the butter and sugar into a bowl and mix well with a wooden spoon, then beat in the egg yolk and lemon juice. Sift together the flour and a pinch of salt into the mixture, add the candied peel and candied cherries, and stir until thoroughly combined. Halve the dough, shape into balls, wrap in plastic wrap, and chill in the refrigerator for 30–60 minutes.

2. Preheat the oven to 375°F/190°C. Generously grease round-based muffin pans with butter.

3. Unwrap the dough and roll out between 2 sheets of baking parchment. Stamp out cookies with a 2¾–3½-inch/7–8-cm sun-shaped cutter and put them in the prepared pans.

4. Bake for 10–15 minutes, until light golden brown. Let cool in the pans.

5. Sift the confectioners' sugar into a bowl, add the food coloring and stir in just enough water to give the frosting the consistency of thick cream. Put the cookies on wire racks and gently spread the frosting on them. When it is just beginning to set, gently press 3–4 eggs into each and sprinkle the sugar sprinkles around them. Let set completely.

Makes about 20–25

* 1 cup butter, softened, plus extra for greasing
* scant ¾ cup superfine sugar
* 1 egg yolk, lightly beaten
  2 tsp lemon juice
* 2½ cups all-purpose flour
  1 tbsp chopped candied peel
  ¼ cup finely chopped candied cherries
* salt

To decorate
1¾ cups confectioners' sugar
few drops of edible yellow food coloring
mini sugar-coated Easter eggs
yellow sugar sprinkles

Easter Bunny Cookies

1. Put the butter and sugar into a bowl and mix well with a wooden spoon, then beat in the egg yolk and vanilla extract. Sift together the flour, unsweetened cocoa powder, and a pinch of salt into the mixture, add the ginger, and stir until thoroughly combined. Halve the dough, shape into balls, wrap in plastic wrap, and chill in the refrigerator for 30–60 minutes.

2. Preheat the oven to 375°F/190°C. Line 2 cookie sheets with baking parchment.

3. Unwrap the dough and roll out between 2 sheets of baking parchment. Stamp out 15 cookies with a 2-inch/5-cm plain cutter (bodies), 15 cookies with a 1¼-inch/3-cm plain cutter (heads), 30 cookies with a ¾-inch/2-cm plain cutter (ears), and 15 cookies with a ½-inch/1-cm plain cutter (tails). Make up the bunnies on the cookie sheets spaced well apart. Piece together.

4. Bake for 7 minutes, then brush the bunnies with egg white and sprinkle with superfine sugar. Return to the oven and bake for 5–8 minutes. Remove from the oven and put a mini marshmallow in the center of each tail. Return to the oven for 1 minute. Let cool for 5–10 minutes, then transfer to wire racks to cool completely. Sift the confectioners' sugar into a bowl and stir in enough water to give the frosting the consistency of thick cream. Add the food coloring and decorate. Let set.

Makes about 15

- 1 cup butter, softened
- scant ¾ cup superfine sugar, plus extra for sprinkling
- 1 egg yolk, lightly beaten
- 2 tsp vanilla extract
- 2¼ cups all-purpose flour
- ¼ cup unsweetened cocoa powder
- 2 tbsp finely chopped preserved ginger
- 1 egg white, lightly beaten
- 15 white mini marshmallows
- 1¼ cups confectioners' sugar
- few drops of edible food coloring
- salt

57

Traditional Easter Cookies

1. Put the butter and sugar into a bowl and mix well with a wooden spoon, then beat in the egg yolk. Sift together the flour, apple pie spice, and a pinch of salt into the mixture, add the candied peel and currants, and stir until thoroughly combined. Halve the dough, shape into balls, wrap in plastic wrap, and chill in the refrigerator for 30–60 minutes.

2. Preheat the oven to 375°F/190°C. Line 2 cookie sheets with baking parchment.

3. Unwrap the dough and roll out between 2 sheets of baking parchment. Stamp out cookies with a 2½-inch/6-cm fluted round cutter and put them on the prepared cookie sheets spaced well apart.

4. Bake for 7 minutes, then brush with the egg white, and sprinkle with superfine sugar. Return to the oven and bake for 5–8 minutes more, until light golden brown. Let cool on the cookie sheets for 5–10 minutes, then using a metal spatula, carefully transfer to wire racks to cool completely.

Makes about 30

* 1 cup butter, softened
* scant ¾ cup superfine sugar, plus extra for sprinkling
* 1 egg yolk, lightly beaten
* 2½ cups all-purpose flour
* 1 tsp apple pie spice
* 1 tbsp candied peel
* ¼ cup currants
* 1 egg white, lightly beaten
* salt

Halloween Spider's Web Cookies

1. Put the butter and sugar into a bowl and mix, then beat in the egg yolk and peppermint extract. Sift together the flour, unsweetened cocoa powder, and a pinch of salt into the mixture and stir until thoroughly combined. Halve the dough, shape into balls, wrap in plastic wrap, and chill in the refrigerator for 30–60 minutes.

2. Preheat the oven to 375°F/190°C. Line 2 cookie sheets with baking parchment.

3. Unwrap the dough and roll out between 2 sheets of baking parchment. Stamp out cookies with a 2½-inch/6-cm plain round cutter and put them on the prepared cookie sheets spaced well apart.

4. Bake for 10–15 minutes, until light golden brown. Let cool for 5–10 minutes, then transfer to wire racks to cool.

5. Sift the confectioners' sugar into a bowl, add the vanilla extract, and stir in the hot water until the frosting is smooth and has the consistency of thick cream. With the cookies still on the racks, spread most of the white frosting over them. Add a few drops of black food coloring to the remaining frosting and spoon it into a pastry bag with a fine tip. Starting from the middle of the cookie, pipe a series of concentric circles. Then carefully draw a toothpick through the frosting from the middle to the outside edge to divide the cookie first into quarters and then into eighths. Repeat with the remaining cookies. Let set.

Makes about 30

* 1 cup butter, softened
* scant ¾ cup superfine sugar
* 1 egg yolk, lightly beaten
  1 tsp peppermint extract
* 2¼ cups all-purpose flour
  ¼ cup unsweetened cocoa powder
* salt

To decorate
1½ cups confectioners' sugar
few drops vanilla extract
1–1½ tbsp hot water
few drops of edible black food coloring

133

Christmas Angels

① Put the butter and sugar into a bowl and mix well with a wooden spoon, then beat in the egg yolk and passion fruit pulp. Sift together the flour and a pinch of salt into the mixture, add the coconut, and stir until thoroughly combined. Halve the dough, shape into balls, wrap in plastic wrap, and chill in the refrigerator for 30–60 minutes.

② Preheat the oven to 375°F/190°C. Line 2 cookie sheets with baking parchment.

③ Unwrap the dough and roll out between 2 sheets of baking parchment. Stamp out cookies with a 2¾-inch/7-cm angel-shaped cutter and put them on the prepared cookie sheets spaced well apart.

④ Bake for 10–15 minutes, until light golden brown. Let cool on the cookie sheets for 5–10 minutes, then using a metal spatula, carefully transfer to wire racks to cool completely.

⑤ Sift the confectioners' sugar into a bowl and stir in the passion fruit pulp until the frosting has the consistency of thick cream. With the cookies still on the racks, spread the frosting over them. Sprinkle with the edible glitter and let set.

Makes about 25

✳ 1 cup butter, softened
✳ scant ¾ cup superfine sugar
✳ 1 egg yolk, lightly beaten
2 tsp passion fruit pulp
✳ 2½ cups all-purpose flour
⅔ cup unsweetened dried coconut
✳ salt

To decorate
1½ cups confectioners' sugar
1–1½ tbsp passion fruit pulp
edible silver glitter, for sprinkling

60

Christmas Bells

1. Put the butter, sugar, and lemon rind into a bowl and mix well with a wooden spoon, then beat in the egg yolk. Sift together the flour, cinnamon, and a pinch of salt into the mixture, add the chocolate chips, and stir until thoroughly combined. Halve the dough, shape into balls, wrap in plastic wrap, and chill in the refrigerator for 30–60 minutes.

2. Preheat the oven to 375°F/190°C. Line 2 cookie sheets with baking parchment.

3. Unwrap the dough and roll out between 2 sheets of baking parchment. Stamp out cookies with a 2-in/5-cm bell-shaped cutter and put them on the prepared cookie sheets spaced well apart.

4. Bake for 10–15 minutes, until light golden brown. Let cool on the cookie sheets for 5–10 minutes, then using a metal spatula, carefully transfer to wire racks to cool completely.

5. Combine the egg white and lemon juice in a bowl, then gradually beat in the confectioners' sugar until smooth. With the cookies still on the racks, spread the frosting over them. Place a silver ball on the clapper shape at the bottom of the cookie and let set completely. When the frosting is dry, use the food coloring pens to draw patterns on the cookies.

Makes about 30

* 1 cup butter, softened
* scant ¾ cup superfine sugar
  finely grated rind of 1 lemon
* 1 egg yolk, lightly beaten
* 2½ cups all-purpose flour
  ½ tsp ground cinnamon
  generous ½ cup semisweet
  chocolate chips
* salt

To decorate
2 tbsp lightly beaten egg white
2 tbsp lemon juice
2 cups confectioners' sugar
30 silver balls
food coloring pens

61

Christmas Tree Decorations

1. Put the butter and sugar into a bowl and mix, then beat in the egg yolk and vanilla extract. Sift together the flour and a pinch of salt into the mixture and stir until thoroughly combined. Halve the dough, shape into balls, wrap in plastic wrap, and chill in the refrigerator for 30–60 minutes.

2. Preheat the oven to 375°F/190°C. Line 2 cookie sheets with baking parchment.

3. Unwrap the dough and roll out between 2 sheets of baking parchment. Stamp out cookies with Christmas-themed cutters and put them on the prepared cookie sheets spaced well apart. Using the end of a large plain piping tip, stamp out rounds from each shape and remove them. Make a small hole in the top of each cookie with a skewer so that they can be threaded with ribbon.

4. Meanwhile, lightly crush the candies by tapping them with a rolling pin. Unwrap and sort into separate bowls by color.

5. Remove the cookies from the oven and fill the holes with the crushed candies. Return to the oven and bake for 5–8 minutes more, until the cookies are light golden brown and the candies have melted and filled the holes. If the holes for hanging the cookies have closed up, pierce them again with the skewer while the cookies are still warm. If there are any gaps in the cookies, gently spread the melted candies with the skewer to fill. Let cool completely on the cookie sheets. Thread thin ribbon through the holes in the top and hang.

Makes 20–25

* 1 cup butter, softened
* scant ¾ cup superfine sugar
* 1 egg yolk, lightly beaten
* 2 tsp vanilla extract
* 2½ cups all-purpose flour
  1 egg white, lightly beaten
  2 tbsp colored sprinkles
  14 oz/400 g fruit-flavored hard candies in different colors
* salt

Fruity

62

Mixed Fruit Cookies

1. Put the butter and sugar into a bowl and mix well with a wooden spoon, then beat in the egg yolk. Sift together the flour, apple pie spice, and a pinch of salt into the mixture, add the apple, pear, prunes, and orange rind, and stir until thoroughly combined. Shape the dough into a log, wrap in plastic wrap, and chill in the refrigerator for 30–60 minutes.

2. Preheat the oven to 375°F/190°C. Line 2 cookie sheets with baking parchment.

3. Unwrap the log and cut it into ¼-inch/5-mm thick slices with a sharp serrated knife. Put them on the prepared cookie sheets spaced well apart.

4. Bake for 10–15 minutes, until golden brown. Let cool on the cookie sheets for 5–10 minutes, then using a metal spatula, carefully transfer the cookies to wire racks to cool completely.

Makes about 30

* 1 cup butter, softened
* scant ¾ cup superfine sugar
* 1 egg yolk, lightly beaten
* 2½ cups all-purpose flour
* ½ tsp apple pie spice
* ¼ cup chopped plumped dried apple
* ¼ cup chopped plumped dried pear
* ¼ cup chopped plumped prunes
* grated rind of 1 orange
* salt

63

Chocolate & Apricot Cookies

1. Put the butter and sugar into a bowl and mix well with a wooden spoon, then beat in the egg yolk and amaretto liqueur. Sift together the flour and a pinch of salt into the mixture, add the chocolate chips and apricots, and stir until thoroughly combined.

2. Shape the mixture into a log. Spread out the almonds in a shallow dish and roll the log in them to coat. Wrap in plastic wrap and chill in the refrigerator for 30–60 minutes.

3. Preheat the oven to 375°F/190°C. Line 2 cookie sheets with baking parchment.

4. Unwrap the dough and cut into ¼-inch/5-mm slices with a sharp serrated knife. Put them on the prepared cookie sheets spaced well apart.

5. Bake for 12–15 minutes, until golden brown. Let cool on the cookie sheets for 5–10 minutes, then using a metal spatula, carefully transfer to wire racks to cool completely.

Makes about 30

* 1 cup butter, softened
* scant ¾ cup superfine sugar
* 1 egg yolk, lightly beaten
  2 tsp amaretto liqueur
* 2½ cups all-purpose flour
  ⅓ cup bittersweet chocolate chips
  ½ cup chopped plumped dried apricots
  scant 1 cup blanched almonds, chopped
* salt

64

Pear & Pistachio Cookies

1. Preheat the oven to 375°F/190°C. Line 2 cookie sheets with baking parchment.

2. Put the butter and sugar into a bowl and mix well with a wooden spoon, then beat in the egg yolk and vanilla extract. Sift together the flour and a pinch of salt into the mixture, add the pears and chopped pistachios, and stir until thoroughly combined.

3. Scoop up tablespoons of the mixture and roll into balls. Put them on the prepared cookie sheets spaced well apart and flatten slightly. Gently press a whole pistachio into the center of each cookie.

4. Bake for 10–15 minutes, until golden brown. Let cool on the cookie sheets for 5–10 minutes, then using a metal spatula, carefully transfer to wire racks to cool completely.

Makes about 30

- 1 cup butter, softened
- scant ¾ cup superfine sugar
- 1 egg yolk, lightly beaten
- 2 tsp vanilla extract
- 2½ cups all-purpose flour
- ½ cup finely chopped plumped dried pears
- ½ cup pistachios, chopped
- salt
- whole pistachios, to decorate

65

Orange & Lemon Cookies

1. Put the butter and sugar into a bowl and mix well with a wooden spoon, then beat in the egg yolk. Sift together the flour and a pinch of salt into the mixture and stir until thoroughly combined. Halve the dough and gently knead the orange rind into one half and the lemon rind into the other. Shape into balls, wrap in plastic wrap, and chill in the refrigerator for 30–60 minutes.

2. Preheat the oven to 375°F/190°C. Line 2 cookie sheets with baking parchment.

3. Unwrap the orange-flavored dough and roll out between 2 sheets of baking parchment. Stamp out cookies with a 2½-inch/6-cm cookie cutter and put them on a prepared cookie sheet spaced well apart. Repeat with the lemon-flavored dough and stamp out crescents. Put them on the other prepared cookie sheet spaced well apart.

4. Bake for 10–15 minutes, until golden brown. Let cool for 5–10 minutes, then carefully transfer to wire racks to cool completely.

5. To decorate, combine the egg white and lemon juice. Gradually beat in the confectioners' sugar with a wooden spoon until smooth. Spoon half the frosting into another bowl. Stir yellow food coloring into one bowl and orange into the other. With the cookies still on the racks, spread the icing over the cookies and decorate with the jelly slices. Let set.

Makes about 30

* 1 cup butter, softened
* scant ¾ cup superfine sugar
* 1 egg yolk, lightly beaten
* 2½ cups all-purpose flour
  finely grated rind of 1 orange
  finely grated rind of 1 lemon
* salt

To decorate
1 tbsp lightly beaten egg white
1 tbsp lemon juice
1 cup confectioners' sugar
few drops yellow food coloring
few drops orange food coloring
about 15 lemon jelly fruit slices
about 15 orange jelly fruit slices

66

Walnut & Fig Pinwheels

1. Put the butter and scant ¾ cup of the sugar into a bowl and mix well with a wooden spoon, then beat in the egg yolk. Sift together the flour and a pinch of salt into the mixture, add the ground walnuts, and stir until thoroughly combined. Shape the dough into a ball, wrap in plastic wrap, and chill for 30–60 minutes.

2. Meanwhile, put the remaining sugar into a saucepan and stir in ½ cup of water, then add the figs, mint tea, and chopped mint. Bring to a boil, stirring constantly, until the sugar has dissolved, then lower the heat, and simmer gently, stirring occasionally, for 5 minutes. Remove the saucepan from the heat and let cool.

3. Unwrap the dough and roll out between 2 sheets of baking parchment into a 12-inch/30-cm square. Spread the fig filling evenly over the dough, then roll up like a jelly roll. Wrap in plastic wrap and chill in the refrigerator for 30 minutes.

4. Preheat the oven to 375°F/190°C. Line 2 cookie sheets with baking parchment.

5. Unwrap the roll and cut into thin slices with a sharp serrated knife. Put the slices on the prepared cookie sheets spread well apart. Bake for 10–15 minutes, until golden brown. Let cool on the cookie sheets for 5–10 minutes, then using a metal spatula, transfer to wire racks to cool completely.

Makes about 30

* 1 cup butter, softened
* 1 cup superfine sugar
* 1 egg yolk, lightly beaten
* 2 cups all-purpose flour
  ½ cup ground walnuts
  1⅔ cups dried figs, finely chopped
  5 tbsp freshly brewed mint tea
  2 tsp finely chopped fresh mint
* salt

6 7

Banana & Raisin Cookies

1. Put the raisins into a bowl, pour in the orange juice or rum, and let soak for 30 minutes. Drain the raisins, reserving any remaining orange juice or rum.

2. Preheat the oven to 375°F/190°C. Line 2 cookie sheets with baking parchment.

3. Put the butter and sugar into a bowl and mix well with a wooden spoon, then beat in the egg yolk and 2 teaspoons of the reserved orange juice or rum. Sift together the flour and a pinch of salt into the mixture, add the raisins and dried bananas, and stir until thoroughly combined.

4. Put tablespoons of the mixture into heaps on the prepared cookie sheets spaced well apart, then flatten them gently. Bake for 12–15 minutes, until golden. Let cool on the cookie sheets for 5–10 minutes, then using a metal spatula, carefully transfer to wire racks to cool completely.

Makes about 30

scant ¼ cup raisins
½ cup orange juice or rum
* 1 cup butter, softened
* scant ¾ cup superfine sugar
* 1 egg yolk, lightly beaten
* 2½ cups all-purpose flour
3 oz/85 g dried bananas, finely chopped
* salt

Cherry & Chocolate Diamonds

1. Put the butter and sugar into a bowl and mix well with a wooden spoon, then beat in the egg yolk and vanilla extract. Sift together the flour and a pinch of salt into the mixture, add the candied cherries and chocolate chips, and stir until thoroughly combined. Halve the dough, shape into balls, wrap in plastic wrap, and chill in the refrigerator for 30–60 minutes.

2. Preheat the oven to 375°F/190°C. Line 2 cookie sheets with baking parchment.

3. Unwrap the dough and roll out between 2 sheets of baking parchment to about ⅛ inch/3 mm thick. Stamp out cookies with a diamond-shaped cutter and put them on the prepared cookie sheets.

4. Bake for 10–15 minutes, until light golden brown. Let cool on the cookie sheets for 5–10 minutes, then using a metal spatula, carefully transfer to wire racks to cool completely.

Makes about 30

* 1 cup butter, softened
* scant ¾ cup superfine sugar
* 1 egg yolk, lightly beaten
* 2 tsp vanilla extract
* 2½ cups all-purpose flour
  ¼ cup candied cherries, finely chopped
  ⅓ cup milk chocolate chips
* salt

Grapefruit & Apple Mint Cookies

1. Put the butter and sugar into a bowl and mix well with a wooden spoon, then beat in the egg yolk and grapefruit juice. Sift together the flour and a pinch of salt into the mixture, add the grapefruit rind and chopped mint, and stir until thoroughly combined. Halve the dough, shape into balls, wrap in plastic wrap, and chill in the refrigerator for 30–60 minutes.

2. Preheat the oven to 375°F/190°C. Line 2 cookie sheets with baking parchment.

3. Unwrap the dough and roll out between 2 sheets of baking parchment to ⅛ inch/3 mm thick. Stamp out cookies with a 2-inch/5-cm flower cutter and put them on the prepared cookie sheets spaced well apart. Sprinkle with superfine sugar.

4. Bake for 10–15 minutes, until golden brown. Let cool on the cookie sheets for 5–10 minutes, then using a metal spatula, carefully transfer to wire racks to cool completely.

Makes about 30

- 1 cup butter, softened
- scant ¾ cup superfine sugar, plus extra for sprinkling
- 1 egg yolk, lightly beaten
  2 tsp grapefruit juice
- 2½ cups all-purpose flour
  grated rind of 1 grapefruit
  2 tsp finely chopped fresh apple mint
- salt

Lemon & Lime Cookies

1. For the decoration, put the chocolate in a heatproof bowl and melt over a saucepan of gently simmering water. Remove from the heat and let cool slightly. Line a baking sheet with baking parchment. Dip the strips of lime rind into the melted chocolate until well-coated, then put on the prepared sheet to set.

2. Put the butter and sugar into a bowl and mix well with a wooden spoon, then beat in the egg yolk and lime juice. Sift together the flour and a pinch of salt into the mixture, add the lemon rind, and stir until thoroughly combined. Halve the dough, shape into balls, wrap in plastic wrap, and chill in the refrigerator for 30–60 minutes.

3. Preheat the oven to 375°F/190°C. Line 2 cookie sheets with baking parchment.

4. Unwrap the dough and roll out between 2 sheets of baking parchment to ⅛ in/3 mm thick. Stamp out rounds with a 2½-in/6-cm plain cutter and put on the prepared cookie sheets.

5. Bake for 10–15 minutes, until golden brown. Let cool for 5–10 minutes, then carefully transfer to wire racks to cool completely.

6. For the frosting, mix together the egg white and lime juice. Gradually beat in the confectioners' sugar until smooth. Spread the frosting on the cookies and top with the chocolate-coated lime rind. Let set.

Makes about 30

- 1 cup butter, softened
- scant ¾ cup superfine sugar
- 1 egg yolk, lightly beaten
- 2 tsp lime juice
- 2½ cups all-purpose flour
- finely grated rind of 1 lemon
- salt

To decorate
- 5 oz/140 g bittersweet chocolate, broken into pieces
- 30 thinly pared strips of lime rind
- 1 tbsp lightly beaten egg white
- 1 tbsp lime juice
- 1 cup confectioners' sugar

Mango, Coconut & Ginger Cookies

1. Put the butter and sugar into a bowl and mix well with a wooden spoon, then beat in the egg yolk and ginger syrup. Sift together the flour and a pinch of salt into the mixture, add the chopped ginger and mango, and stir until thoroughly combined.

2. Spread out the coconut in a shallow dish. Shape the dough into a log and roll it in the coconut to coat. Wrap in plastic wrap and chill in the refrigerator for 30–60 minutes.

3. Preheat the oven to 375°F/190°C. Line 2 cookie sheets with baking parchment.

4. Unwrap the log and cut it into ¼-inch/5-mm slices with a sharp serrated knife and put them on the prepared cookie sheets spaced well apart.

5. Bake for 12–15 minutes. Let cool on the cookie sheets for 5–10 minutes, then using a metal spatula, carefully transfer to wire racks to cool completely.

Makes about 30

- 1 cup butter, softened
- scant ¾ cup superfine sugar
- 1 egg yolk, lightly beaten
- 4 tbsp chopped preserved ginger, plus 2 tsp syrup from the jar
- 2½ cups all-purpose flour
- ½ cup chopped plumped dried mango
- generous 1 cup unsweetened dried coconut
- salt

72

Strawberry Pinks

1. Preheat the oven to 375°F/190°C. Line 2 cookie sheets with baking parchment.

2. Put the butter and sugar into a bowl and mix well with a wooden spoon, then beat in the egg yolk and strawberry flavoring. Sift together the flour and a pinch of salt into the mixture, add the coconut, and stir until thoroughly combined.

3. Scoop up tablespoons of the mixture and roll them into balls. Put on the prepared cookie sheets spaced well apart and use the handle of a dampened wooden spoon to make a hollow in the center of each. Fill the hollows with strawberry jam.

4. Bake for 12–15 minutes. Let cool on the cookie sheets for 5–10 minutes, then using a metal spatula, carefully transfer the cookies to wire racks to cool completely.

Makes about 30

* 1 cup butter, softened
* scant ¾ cup superfine sugar
* 1 egg yolk, lightly beaten
  1 tsp strawberry flavoring
* 2½ cups all-purpose flour
  generous 1 cup unsweetened dried coconut
  4 tbsp strawberry jam
* salt

73

Apple Suns & Pear Stars

1. Put the butter and sugar into a bowl and mix well with a wooden spoon, then beat in the egg yolk. Sift together the flour and a pinch of salt into the mixture and stir until thoroughly combined. Transfer half the dough to another bowl.

2. Add the apple pie spice and dried apple to one bowl and mix well. Shape into a ball, wrap in plastic wrap, and chill in the refrigerator for 30–60 minutes. Add the ginger and dried pears to the other bowl and mix well. Shape into a ball, wrap in plastic wrap, and chill in the refrigerator for 30–60 minutes.

3. Preheat the oven to 375°F/190°C. Line 2 cookie sheets with baking parchment.

4. Unwrap the apple-flavored dough and roll out between 2 sheets of baking parchment to about ⅛ inch/3 mm thick. Stamp out cookies with a sun-shaped cutter and put them on a prepared cookie sheet. Repeat with the pear-flavored dough and stamp out cookies with a star-shaped cutter. Put them on the other prepared cookie sheet.

5. Bake for 5 minutes, then remove the star-shaped cookies from the oven and sprinkle with the sliced almonds. Return to the oven and bake for 5–10 minutes. Remove the cookies from the oven but do not turn off the heat. Brush the apple suns with a little egg white and sprinkle with the turbinado sugar. Return to the oven for 2–3 minutes. Let all the cookies cool for 5–10 minutes, then carefully transfer them to wire racks to cool completely.

Makes about 30

* 1 cup butter, softened
* scant ¾ cup superfine sugar
* 1 egg yolk, lightly beaten
* 2½ cups all-purpose flour
* ½ tsp apple pie spice
* ½ cup finely chopped plumped dried apple
* ½ tsp ground ginger
* ½ cup finely chopped plumped dried pears
* ¼ cup sliced almonds
* 1 egg white, lightly beaten
* turbinado sugar, for sprinkling
* salt

165

74

Coconut & Cranberry Cookies

1. Preheat the oven to 375°F/190°C. Line 2 cookie sheets with baking parchment.

2. Put the butter and sugar into a bowl and mix well with a wooden spoon, then beat in the egg yolk and vanilla extract. Sift together the flour and a pinch of salt into the mixture, add the coconut and cranberries, and stir until thoroughly combined. Scoop up tablespoons of the dough and place in mounds on the prepared cookie sheets spaced well apart.

3. Bake for 12–15 minutes, until golden brown. Let cool on the cookie sheets for 5–10 minutes, then using a metal spatula, carefully transfer to wire racks to cool completely.

Makes about 30

* 1 cup butter, softened
* scant ¾ cup superfine sugar
* 1 egg yolk, lightly beaten
* 2 tsp vanilla extract
* 2½ cups all-purpose flour
  ½ cup unsweetened dried coconut
  ½ cup dried cranberries
* salt

75

Blueberry & Orange Cookies

1. Put the butter and sugar into a bowl and mix well with a wooden spoon, then beat in the egg yolk and orange extract. Sift together the flour and a pinch of salt into the mixture, add the blueberries, and stir until thoroughly combined. Shape the dough into a log, wrap in plastic wrap, and chill in the refrigerator for 30–60 minutes.

2. Preheat the oven to 375°F/190°C. Line 2 cookie sheets with baking parchment.

3. Unwrap the log and cut into ¼-inch/5-mm slices with a sharp serrated knife. Put them on the prepared cookie sheets spaced well apart.

4. Bake for 10–15 minutes, until golden brown. Let cool on the cookie sheets for 5–10 minutes, then using a metal spatula, carefully transfer to wire racks to cool completely.

5. Just before serving, beat the cream cheese in a bowl and stir in the orange rind. Spread the mixture over the cookies and sprinkle with the chopped nuts.

Makes about 30

* 1 cup butter, softened
* scant ¾ cup superfine sugar
* 1 egg yolk, lightly beaten
  1 tsp orange extract
* 2½ cups all-purpose flour
  scant 1 cup dried blueberries
  scant ½ cup cream cheese
  grated rind of 1 orange
  ⅓ cup finely chopped
    macadamia nuts
* salt

Blueberry & Cranberry Cinnamon Cookies

1. Preheat the oven to 375°F/190°C. Line 2 cookie sheets with baking parchment.

2. Put the butter and sugar into a bowl and mix well with a wooden spoon, then beat in the egg yolk and vanilla extract. Sift together the flour, cinnamon, and a pinch of salt into the mixture, add the blueberries and cranberries, and stir until thoroughly combined.

3. Spread out the pine nuts in a shallow dish. Scoop up tablespoons of the mixture and roll them into balls. Roll the balls in the pine kernels to coat, then place on the prepared cookie sheets spaced well apart and flatten slightly.

4. Bake for 10–15 minutes. Let cool on the cookie sheets for 5–10 minutes, then using a metal spatula, carefully transfer the cookies to wire racks to cool completely.

Makes about 30

* 1 cup butter, softened
* scant ¾ cup superfine sugar
* 1 egg yolk, lightly beaten
* 2 tsp vanilla extract
* 2½ cups all-purpose flour
  1 tsp ground cinnamon
  ½ cup dried blueberries
  ½ cup dried cranberries
  ½ cup pine nuts, chopped
* salt

Date & Lemon Spirals

1. Put the butter and scant ¾ cup of the sugar into a bowl and mix well with a wooden spoon, then beat in the egg yolk and lemon extract. Sift together the flour and a pinch of salt into the mixture and stir until thoroughly combined. Shape the dough into a ball, wrap in plastic wrap, and chill in the refrigerator for 30–60 minutes.

2. Meanwhile, put the dates, honey, lemon juice, and lemon rind in a saucepan and stir in ½ cup of water. Bring to a boil, stirring constantly, then lower the heat and simmer gently, stirring occasionally, for 5 minutes. Remove from the heat and let cool, then chill in the refrigerator for 15 minutes.

3. Combine the cinnamon and remaining sugar in a bowl. Unwrap the dough and roll out between 2 sheets of baking parchment into a 12-inch/30-cm square. Sprinkle the cinnamon and sugar mixture over the dough and roll lightly with the rolling pin. Spread the date mixture evenly over the dough, then roll up like a jelly roll. Wrap in plastic wrap and chill in the refrigerator for 30 minutes.

4. Preheat the oven to 375°F/190°C. Line 2 cookie sheets with baking parchment. Unwrap the roll and cut into thin slices with a sharp serrated knife. Put them on the prepared cookie sheets spaced well apart. Bake for 12–15 minutes.

Makes about 30

* 1 cup butter, softened
* scant 1 cup superfine sugar
* 1 egg yolk, lightly beaten
  1 tsp lemon extract
* 2½ cups all-purpose flour
  1⅔ cups pitted and finely chopped dried dates
  2 tbsp lemon blossom honey
  5 tbsp lemon juice
  1 tbsp finely grated lemon rind
  1 tsp ground cinnamon
* salt

78

Plum & White Chocolate Cookies

1. Put the butter and sugar into a bowl and mix well with a wooden spoon, then beat in the egg yolk and vanilla extract. Sift together the flour, unsweetened cocoa, and a pinch of salt into the mixture and stir until thoroughly combined. Halve the dough, shape into balls, wrap in plastic wrap, and chill in the refrigerator for 30–60 minutes.

2. Preheat the oven to 375°F/190°C. Line 2 cookie sheets with baking parchment.

3. Unwrap a ball of dough and roll out between 2 sheets of baking parchment to about ⅛ inch/3 mm thick. Stamp out 15 cookies with a plain 2-inch/5-cm cutter and put them on the prepared cookie sheets spaced well apart. Divide the chopped chocolate among the cookies. Roll out the remaining dough between 2 sheets of baking parchment and stamp out cookies with a 2½–2¾-inch/6–7-cm cutter. Place them on top of the first cookies and press the edges together to seal.

4. Bake for 10–15 minutes, until firm. Let cool for 5–10 minutes, then carefully transfer the cookies to wire racks to cool completely.

5. To decorate, melt the chocolate in a heatproof bowl set over a saucepan of gently simmering water. Remove from the heat and let cool slightly. With the cookies still on the racks, dip the cut sides of the plums into the melted chocolate and stick them in the middle of the cookies. Spoon the remaining melted chocolate over them and let set.

Makes about 30

* 1 cup butter, softened
* scant ¾ cup superfine sugar
* 1 egg yolk, lightly beaten
* 2 tsp vanilla extract
* 2 cups all-purpose flour
  ½ cup unsweetened cocoa powder
  3½ oz/100 g white chocolate, chopped
* salt

To decorate
2 oz/55 g white chocolate, broken into pieces
15 plumped dried plums, halved

Papaya & Cashew Nut Cookies

1. Put the butter and sugar into a bowl and mix well with a wooden spoon, then beat in the egg yolk and lime juice. Sift together the flour and a pinch of salt into the mixture, add the papaya, and stir until thoroughly combined.

2. Spread out the nuts in a shallow dish. Shape the dough into a log and roll in the cashews to coat, then wrap in plastic wrap, and chill in the refrigerator for 30–60 minutes.

3. Preheat the oven to 375°F/190°C. Line 2 cookie sheets with baking parchment.

4. Unwrap the dough and cut into slices with a sharp serrated knife. Put them on the prepared cookie sheets spaced well apart.

5. Bake for 12–15 minutes, until light golden brown. Let cool on the cookie sheets for 5–10 minutes, then using a metal spatula, carefully transfer to wire racks to cool completely.

Makes about 30

- 1 cup butter, softened
- scant ¾ cup superfine sugar
- 1 egg yolk, lightly beaten
- 2 tsp lime juice
- 2½ cups all-purpose flour
- scant 1 cup chopped plumped dried papaya
- ¾ cup finely chopped cashew nuts
- salt

Papaya & Cashew Nut Cookies

1. Put the butter and sugar into a bowl and mix well with a wooden spoon, then beat in the egg yolk and lime juice. Sift together the flour and a pinch of salt into the mixture, add the papaya, and stir until thoroughly combined.

2. Spread out the nuts in a shallow dish. Shape the dough into a log and roll in the cashews to coat, then wrap in plastic wrap, and chill in the refrigerator for 30–60 minutes.

3. Preheat the oven to 375°F/190°C. Line 2 cookie sheets with baking parchment.

4. Unwrap the dough and cut into slices with a sharp serrated knife. Put them on the prepared cookie sheets spaced well apart.

5. Bake for 12–15 minutes, until light golden brown. Let cool on the cookie sheets for 5–10 minutes, then using a metal spatula, carefully transfer to wire racks to cool completely.

Makes about 30

- 1 cup butter, softened
- scant ¾ cup superfine sugar
- 1 egg yolk, lightly beaten
- 2 tsp lime juice
- 2½ cups all-purpose flour
- scant 1 cup chopped plumped dried papaya
- ¾ cup finely chopped cashew nuts
- salt

Oaty Raisin & Hazelnut Cookies

1. Preheat the oven to 375°F/190°C. Line 2 cookie sheets with baking parchment. Put the raisins in a bowl, add the orange juice, and let soak for 10 minutes.

2. Put the butter and sugar into a bowl and mix well with a wooden spoon, then beat in the egg yolk and vanilla extract. Sift together the flour and a pinch of salt into the mixture and add the oats and chopped hazelnuts. Drain the raisins, add them to the mixture, and stir until thoroughly combined.

3. Scoop up tablespoons of the mixture and put them in mounds on the prepared cookie sheets spaced well apart. Flatten slightly and place a whole hazelnut in the center of each cookie.

4. Bake for 12–15 minutes, until golden brown. Let cool on the cookie sheets for 5–10 minutes, then using a metal spatula, carefully transfer the cookies to wire racks to cool completely.

Makes about 30

scant ½ cup raisins, chopped
½ cup orange juice
✳ 1 cup butter, softened
✳ scant ¾ cup superfine sugar
✳ 1 egg yolk, lightly beaten
✳ 2 tsp vanilla extract
✳ 2 cups all-purpose flour
½ cup rolled oats
½ cup chopped hazelnuts
✳ salt
whole hazelnuts, to decorate

Peach, Pear & Plum Cookies

1. Preheat the oven to 375°F/190°C. Line 2 cookie sheets with baking parchment.

2. Put the butter and sugar into a bowl and mix well with a wooden spoon, then beat in the egg yolk and almond extract. Sift together the flour and a pinch of salt into the mixture, add the dried fruit, and stir until thoroughly combined.

3. Scoop up tablespoons of the mixture, roll them into balls, and put on the prepared cookie sheets spaced well apart. Make a hollow in the center of each with the dampened handle of a wooden spoon. Fill the hollows with plum jam.

4. Bake for 12–15 minutes, until light golden brown. Let cool on the cookie sheets for 5–10 minutes, then using a metal spatula, carefully transfer to wire racks to cool completely.

Makes about 30

- 1 cup butter, softened
- scant ¾ cup superfine sugar
- 1 egg yolk, lightly beaten
- 2 tsp almond extract
- 2½ cups all-purpose flour
- ½ cup finely chopped plumped dried peach
- ½ cup finely chopped plumped dried pear
- 4 tbsp plum jam
- salt

Double the Fun

Jam Rings

1. Put the butter and sugar into a bowl and mix well with a wooden spoon, then beat in the egg yolk and vanilla extract. Sift together the flour and a pinch of salt into the mixture and stir until thoroughly combined. Halve the dough, shape into balls, wrap in plastic wrap, and chill in the refrigerator for 30–60 minutes.

2. Preheat the oven to 375°F/190°C. Line 2 cookie sheets with baking parchment.

3. Unwrap the dough and roll out between 2 sheets of baking parchment. Stamp out cookies with a 2¾-inch/7-cm fluted round cutter and put half of them on a prepared cookie sheet spaced well apart. Using a 1½-inch/4-cm plain round cutter, stamp out the centers of the remaining cookies and remove. Put the cookie rings on the other cookie sheet spaced well apart.

4. Bake for 7 minutes, then brush the cookie rings with beaten egg white and sprinkle with superfine sugar. Bake for 5–8 minutes more, until light golden brown. Let cool on the cookie sheets for 5–10 minutes, then using a metal spatula, carefully transfer to wire racks to cool completely.

5. To make the filling, beat the butter and confectioners' sugar together in a bowl until smooth and combined. Spread the buttercream over the whole cookies and top with a little jam. Place the cookie rings on top and press gently together.

Makes about 15

* 1 cup butter, softened
* scant ¾ cup superfine sugar, plus extra for sprinkling
* 1 egg yolk, lightly beaten
* 2 tsp vanilla extract
* 2½ cups all-purpose flour
* 1 egg white, lightly beaten
* salt

Jam filling
¼ cup butter, softened

scant 1 cup confectioners' sugar

5 tbsp strawberry or raspberry jam

83

Mint Cookies with White Chocolate Ganache

1. Put the butter and sugar into a bowl and mix well with a wooden spoon, then beat in the egg yolk and vanilla extract. Sift together the flour and a pinch of salt into the mixture, add the chocolate and mint sticks, and stir until thoroughly combined. Halve the dough, shape into balls, wrap in plastic wrap, and chill in the refrigerator for 30–60 minutes.

2. Preheat the oven to 375°F/190°C. Line 2 cookie sheets with baking parchment.

3. Unwrap the dough and roll out between 2 sheets of baking parchment. Stamp out cookies with a 2½-inch/6-cm fluted round cutter and put them on the prepared cookie sheets spaced well apart.

4. Bake for 10–15 minutes, until light golden brown. Let cool on the cookie sheets for 5–10 minutes, then using a metal spatula, carefully transfer to wire racks to cool completely.

5. For the ganache, pour the cream into a saucepan, add the chocolate, and melt over a low heat, stirring occasionally, until smooth. Remove the saucepan from the heat and let cool, then chill in the refrigerator until the mixture has a spreadable consistency.

6. Spread the ganache over half the cookies and top with the remaining cookies. Dust with sifted confectioners' sugar.

Makes about 15

* 1 cup butter, softened
* scant ¾ cup superfine sugar
* 1 egg yolk, lightly beaten
* 2 tsp vanilla extract
* 2½ cups all-purpose flour
  3½ oz/100 g chocolate and mint sticks, finely chopped
* salt
  confectioners' sugar, for dusting

White chocolate ganache
2 tbsp heavy cream
3½ oz/100 g white chocolate, broken into pieces

84

Almond Cookies with Green Tea Cream

1. Mix the butter and sugar, then beat in the egg yolk and vanilla extract. Sift in the flour and a pinch of salt and stir well. Halve the dough, wrap, and chill for 30–60 minutes.

2. Preheat the oven to 375°F/190°C. Line 2 cookie sheets with baking parchment.

3. Roll out a dough ball between sheets of baking parchment. Stamp out cookies with a 2½-inch/6-cm cutter and put on a cookie sheet. Roll out the other ball of dough to ½ inch/ 1 cm thick. Sprinkle with the almonds, cover again with baking parchment, and roll out to ¼ inch/5 mm thick. Stamp out 2½-inch/6-cm cookies and put on the other cookie sheet. Brush with egg white and sprinkle with sugar. Bake for 10–15 minutes, until golden. Cool for 5–10 minutes, then transfer to wire racks.

4. For the green tea cream, bring the milk to a boil, then remove from the heat. Add the tea, cover the surface of the milk with plastic wrap, and let steep for 15 minutes. Strain into a clean saucepan. Stir in the sugar and pudding mix and bring to a boil, stirring until thickened. Remove from the heat, cover the surface with plastic wrap, and let cool.

5. Beat the cream cheese until smooth. Beat in the green tea mixture. Spread the cream over the plain cookies and top with the almond cookies.

Makes about 15

* 1 cup butter, softened
* scant ¾ cup superfine sugar, plus extra for sprinkling
* 1 egg yolk, lightly beaten
* 2 tsp vanilla extract
* 2 cups all-purpose flour
  ¼ cup slivered almonds
  1 egg white, lightly beaten
* salt

Green tea cream
½ cup milk
2 tsp (2 tea bags) green tea leaves
1 tbsp superfine sugar
1 tbsp pudding mix
generous ½ cup cream cheese

85

Apple & Spice Cookies

1. Put the butter and sugar into a bowl and mix well with a wooden spoon, then beat in the egg yolk and apple juice. Sift together the flour, cinnamon, apple pie spice, and a pinch of salt into the mixture, add the dried apple, and stir until thoroughly combined. Halve the dough, shape into balls, wrap in plastic wrap, and chill in the refrigerator for 30–60 minutes.

2. Preheat the oven to 375°F/190°C. Line 2 cookie sheets with baking parchment.

3. Unwrap the dough and roll out between 2 sheets of baking parchment. Stamp out cookies with a 2-inch/5-cm square cutter and put them on the prepared cookie sheets spaced well apart.

4. Bake for 10–15 minutes, until light golden brown. Let cool on the cookie sheets for 5–10 minutes, then using a metal spatula, carefully transfer to wire racks to cool completely.

5. To make the filling, combine the superfine sugar, pudding mix, and milk in a saucepan and bring to a boil, stirring constantly. Cook, stirring constantly, until thickened, then remove the saucepan from the heat and stir in the apple sauce. Cover the surface with plastic wrap and let cool.

6. Spread the filling over half the cookies and top with the remainder.

Makes about 30

* 1 cup butter, softened
* scant ¾ cup superfine sugar
* 1 egg yolk, lightly beaten
  2 tsp apple juice
* 2½ cups all-purpose flour
  ½ tsp ground cinnamon
  ½ tsp apple pie spice
  scant 1 cup finely chopped
    plumped dried apple
* salt

Apple filling
1 tbsp superfine sugar
1 tbsp pudding mix
½ cup milk
5 tbsp apple sauce

Plum & Vanilla Cream Cookies

1. Put the butter and sugar into a bowl and mix well with a wooden spoon, then beat in the egg yolk and vanilla extract. Sift together the flour, pudding mix, and a pinch of salt into the mixture, add the plums, and stir until thoroughly combined. Halve the dough, shape into balls, wrap in plastic wrap, and chill in the refrigerator for 30–60 minutes.

2. Preheat the oven to 375°F/190°C. Line 2 cookie sheets with baking parchment.

3. Unwrap the dough and roll out between 2 sheets of baking parchment. Stamp out cookies with a 2½-inch/6-cm fluted round cutter and put them on the prepared cookie sheets spaced well apart. Using a small diamond-shaped cutter, stamp out the centers of half the cookies and remove.

4. Bake for 10–15 minutes, until light golden brown. Let cool on the cookie sheets for 5–10 minutes, then using a metal spatula, carefully transfer to wire racks to cool completely.

5. To make the vanilla cream, melt the butter in a small saucepan, then remove from the heat. Sift the confectioners' sugar into the saucepan, add the milk and vanilla extract, and beat well until smooth and thoroughly combined. Spread the vanilla cream over the whole cookies and top with the cutout cookies.

Makes about 15

* 1 cup butter, softened
* scant ¾ cup superfine sugar
* 1 egg yolk, lightly beaten
* 2 tsp vanilla extract
* 1½ cups all-purpose flour
  1 cup instant pudding mix
  1 cup finely chopped plumped dried plums
* salt

Vanilla cream
2 tbsp butter
2 cups confectioners' sugar
2 tbsp milk
few drops of vanilla extract

Rum & Raisin Cookies with Orange Filling

① Put the raisins in to a bowl, pour in the rum, and let soak for 15 minutes, then drain reserving any remaining rum. Preheat the oven to 375°F/190°C. Line 2 cookie sheets with baking parchment.

② Put the butter and sugar into a bowl and mix well with a wooden spoon, then beat in the egg yolk and 2 teaspoons of the reserved rum. Sift together the flour and a pinch of salt into the mixture, add the raisins, and stir until thoroughly combined.

③ Scoop up tablespoons of the dough and put them on the prepared cookie sheets spaced well apart. Flatten gently and smooth the tops with the back of a spoon.

④ Bake for 10–15 minutes, until light golden brown. Let cool on the cookie sheets for 5–10 minutes, then using a metal spatula, carefully transfer to wire racks to cool completely.

⑤ To make the filling, sift the confectioners' sugar into a bowl, add the butter, orange rind, rum, and food coloring, if using, and beat well until smooth. Spread the filling over half the cookies and top with the remaining cookies.

Makes about 30

⅔ cup raisins
⅔ cup rum
✳ 1 cup butter, softened
✳ scant ¾ cup superfine sugar
✳ 1 egg yolk, lightly beaten
✳ 2½ cups all-purpose flour
✳ salt

Orange filling
1½ cups confectioners' sugar
6 tbsp butter, softened
2 tsp finely grated orange rind
1 tsp rum
few drops of yellow edible food coloring (optional)

Red Currant & Pastry Cream Cookies

① Mix the butter and sugar, then beat in the egg yolk and vanilla extract. Sift in the flour and a pinch of salt and stir. Halve the dough, wrap, and chill for 45 minutes.

② Preheat the oven to 375°F/190°C. Line 2 cookie sheets with baking parchment.

③ Roll out the dough between sheets of baking parchment. Stamp out cookies with a 2½-inch/6-cm cutter, put on the cookie sheets, and bake for 12 minutes, until golden. Cool for 5 minutes, then transfer to wire racks.

④ For the pastry cream, beat the egg yolk and sugar. Sift in the cornstarch and flour and beat well. Stir in 3 tablespoons of the milk and the vanilla extract. Bring the remaining milk to a boil, then whisk it into the mixture. Return to the saucepan and bring to a boil, stirring. Remove from the heat and beat until cool.

⑤ Stiffly whisk the egg white. Spoon a little egg-yolk mixture into a bowl and stir, fold in the egg white, then fold into the remaining egg-yolk mixture. Heat for 2 minutes, stirring. Let cool. Meanwhile, dip the red currants into the egg white and roll in the superfine sugar. Let dry. Sandwich the cookies together with the pastry cream. Sift the confectioners' sugar into a bowl, stir in the lemon extract and enough warm water to make a smooth frosting. Spread it on the cookies and decorate with red currants.

Makes about 15

✴ 1 cup butter, softened
✴ scant ¾ cup superfine sugar
✴ 1 egg yolk, lightly beaten
✴ 2 tsp vanilla extract
✴ 2½ cups all-purpose flour
✴ salt

Pastry cream
2 egg yolks, lightly beaten
4 tbsp superfine sugar
1 tbsp cornstarch
1 heaping tbsp all-purpose flour
1¼ cups milk
few drops of vanilla extract
1 egg white

To decorate
15 small bunches of red currants
1 egg white, lightly beaten
2–3 tbsp superfine sugar
2 cups confectioners' sugar
¼ tsp lemon extract
2 tbsp warm water

Coffee Cream & Walnut Cookies

1. Put the butter and sugar into a bowl and mix well with a wooden spoon, then beat in the egg yolk and vanilla extract. Sift together the flour and a pinch of salt into the mixture, add the ground walnuts, and stir until thoroughly combined. Halve the dough, shape into balls, wrap in plastic wrap, and chill in the refrigerator for 30–60 minutes.

2. Preheat the oven to 375°F/190°C. Line 2 cookie sheets with baking parchment.

3. Unwrap the dough and roll out between 2 sheets of baking parchment. Stamp out cookies with a 2½-inch/6-cm fluted round cutter and put them on the prepared cookie sheets spaced well apart.

4. Bake for 10–15 minutes, until light golden brown. Let cool on the cookie sheets for 5–10 minutes, then using a metal spatula, carefully transfer to wire racks to cool completely.

5. To make the cream, beat the butter and confectioners' sugar together until smooth and thoroughly combined, then beat in the coffee. Sandwich the cookies together in pairs with the coffee cream, then press together gently so that the cream oozes out of the sides. Smooth the sides with a dampened finger. Spread out the chopped walnuts in a shallow dish and roll the cookies in them to coat the sides of the coffee cream filling. Dust the tops with sifted confectioners' sugar.

Makes about 30

* 1 cup butter, softened
* scant ¾ cup superfine sugar
* 1 egg yolk, lightly beaten
* 2 tsp vanilla extract
* 2 cups all-purpose flour
  ½ cup ground walnuts
  ½ cup finely chopped walnuts,
* salt
  confectioners' sugar,
    for dusting

Coffee cream
6 tbsp butter, softened
¾ cup confectioners' sugar
1½ tsp strong black coffee

Pineapple & Ginger Creams

1. Put the butter and sugar into a bowl and mix well with a wooden spoon, then beat in the egg yolk and vanilla extract. Sift together the flour and a pinch of salt into the mixture, add the pineapple, and stir until thoroughly combined. Halve the dough, shape into balls, wrap in plastic wrap, and chill in the refrigerator for 30–60 minutes.

2. Preheat the oven to 375°F/190°C. Line 2 cookie sheets with baking parchment.

3. Unwrap the dough and roll out between 2 sheets of baking parchment. Stamp out cookies with a 2½-in/6-cm fluted round cutter and put them on the prepared cookie sheets spaced well apart.

4. Bake for 10–15 minutes, until light golden brown. Let cool on the cookie sheets for 5–10 minutes, then using a metal spatula, carefully transfer to wire racks to cool completely.

5. To make the ginger cream, beat the yogurt, syrup, and ginger in a bowl until thoroughly combined. Sandwich the cookies together with the ginger cream. Cover half of each cookie with a piece of paper and dust the exposed half with sifted unsweetened cocoa powder. Cover the cocoa-dusted half of each cookie with a piece of paper and dust the exposed half with sifted confectioners' sugar.

Makes about 15

* 1 cup butter, softened
* scant ¾ cup superfine sugar
* 1 egg yolk, lightly beaten
* 2 tsp vanilla extract
* 2½ cups all-purpose flour
  scant 1 cup finely chopped plumped dried pineapple
* salt
  unsweetened cocoa powder, for dusting
  confectioners' sugar, for dusting

Ginger cream
⅔ cup strained plain yogurt
1 tbsp light corn syrup
1 tbsp ground ginger

91

Crunchy Nut & Honey Sandwich Cookies

① Preheat the oven to 375°F/190°C. Line 2 cookie sheets with baking parchment.

② Put 1 cup of the butter and the superfine sugar into a bowl and mix well with a wooden spoon, then beat in the egg yolk and vanilla extract. Sift together the flour and a pinch of salt into the mixture and stir until thoroughly combined.

③ Scoop up tablespoons of the dough and roll into balls. Put half of them on a prepared cookie sheet spaced well apart and flatten gently. Spread out the nuts in a shallow dish and dip one side of the remaining dough balls into them, then place on the other cookie sheet, nut side uppermost, and flatten gently.

④ Bake for 10–15 minutes, until light golden brown. Let cool on the cookie sheets for 5–10 minutes, then using a metal spatula, carefully transfer to wire racks to cool completely.

⑤ Beat the remaining butter with the confectioners' sugar and honey until creamy and thoroughly mixed. Spread the honey mixture over the plain cookies and top with the nut-coated cookies.

Makes about 30

✳ 1⅓ cups butter, softened
✳ scant ¾ cup superfine sugar
✳ 1 egg yolk, lightly beaten
✳ 2 tsp vanilla extract
✳ 2½ cups all-purpose flour
⅓ cup macadamia nuts, cashew nuts, or pine nuts, chopped
¾ cup confectioners' sugar
⅓ cup clover or other set honey
✳ salt

92

Hearts & Diamonds

1. Put the butter and sugar into a bowl and mix, then beat in the egg yolk and vanilla extract. Sift together the flour and a pinch of salt into the mixture, add the chocolate chips, and stir until thoroughly combined. Halve the dough, shape into balls, wrap in plastic wrap, and chill in the refrigerator for 30–60 minutes.

2. Preheat the oven to 375°F/190°C. Line 2 cookie sheets with baking parchment.

3. Unwrap the dough and roll out between 2 sheets of baking parchment. Stamp out cookies with a 2½-inch/6-cm square fluted cutter and put half of them on a prepared cookie sheet spaced well apart. Using small heart- and diamond-shaped cutters, stamp out the centers of the remaining cookies and remove them. Put the cookies on the other cookie sheet spaced well apart.

4. Bake for 10–15 minutes, until light golden brown. Let cool for 5–10 minutes, then carefully transfer to wire racks to cool completely. To make the filling, put the jelly and lemon juice in a small saucepan and heat gently until the mixture is runny, then boil for 3 minutes. Remove the saucepan from the heat and let cool. Meanwhile, put the cheese, cream, sifted confectioners' sugar, and vanilla extract in a bowl and beat well until thoroughly combined. Spread the cream mixture over the whole cookies, add a little jelly, and top with the cutout cookies.

Makes about 15

* 1 cup butter, softened
* scant ¾ cup superfine sugar
* 1 egg yolk, lightly beaten
* 2 tsp vanilla extract
* 2½ cups all-purpose flour
  generous ½ cup white chocolate chips
* salt

Jelly filling
5–6 tbsp red currant or cranberry jelly
½ tsp lemon juice
⅓ cup farmer's cheese
2 tbsp heavy cream
2 tsp confectioners' sugar
few drops of vanilla extract

Clubs & Spades

1. Put the butter and sugar into a bowl and mix well with a wooden spoon, then beat in the egg yolk and vanilla extract. Sift together the flour and a pinch of salt into the mixture, add the chocolate chips, and stir until thoroughly combined. Halve the dough, shape into balls, wrap in plastic wrap, and chill in the refrigerator for 30–60 minutes.

2. Preheat the oven to 375°F/190°C. Line 2 cookie sheets with baking parchment.

3. Unwrap the dough and roll out between 2 sheets of baking parchment. Stamp out cookies with a 2½-in/6-cm square fluted cutter and put half of them on a prepared cookie sheet spaced well apart. Using small club- and spade-shaped cutters, stamp out the centers of the remaining cookies and remove them. Put the cookies on the other cookie sheet spaced well apart.

4. Bake for 10–15 minutes, until light golden brown. Let cool on the cookie sheets for 5–10 minutes, then using a metal spatula, carefully transfer to wire racks to cool completely.

5. To make the filling, put the butter and syrup into a bowl and sift in the confectioners' sugar and unsweetened cocoa powder. Beat well until smooth. Spread the chocolate cream over the whole cookies and top with the cutout cookies.

Makes about 15

* 1 cup butter, softened
* scant ¾ cup superfine sugar
* 1 egg yolk, lightly beaten
* 2 tsp vanilla extract
* 2½ cups all-purpose flour
  generous ½ cup semisweet chocolate chips
* salt

Filling
¼ cup butter, softened
1 tsp light corn syrup
¾ cup confectioners' sugar
1 tbsp unsweetened cocoa powder

Chocolate & Orange Cookie Sandwiches

1. Preheat the oven to 375°F/190°C. Line 2 cookie sheets with baking parchment.

2. Put the butter, sugar, and orange rind into a bowl and mix well with a wooden spoon, then beat in the egg yolk and vanilla extract. Sift together the flour, unsweetened cocoa powder, and a pinch of salt into the mixture, add the chopped chocolate, and stir until thoroughly combined.

3. Scoop up tablespoons of the dough, roll into balls, and put on the prepared cookie sheets spaced well apart. Gently flatten and smooth the tops with the back of a spoon.

4. Bake for 10–15 minutes, until light golden brown. Let cool on the cookie sheets for 5–10 minutes, then using a metal spatula, carefully transfer to wire racks to cool completely.

5. To make the filling, bring the cream to a boil in a small saucepan, then remove the saucepan from the heat. Stir in the chocolate until the mixture is smooth, then stir in the orange extract. When the mixture is completely cool, use to sandwich the cookies together in pairs.

Makes about 15

* 1 cup butter, softened
* scant ¾ cup superfine sugar
  2 tsp finely grated orange rind
* 1 egg yolk, lightly beaten
* 2 tsp vanilla extract
* 2¼ cups all-purpose flour
  ¼ cup unsweetened cocoa powder
  3½ oz/100 g plain chocolate, finely chopped
* salt

Chocolate filling
½ cup heavy cream
7 oz/200 g white chocolate, broken into pieces
1 tsp orange extract

95

Marshmallow S'mores

1. Put the butter, sugar, and orange rind into a bowl and mix well with a wooden spoon, then beat in the egg yolk. Sift together the flour, unsweetened cocoa powder, cinnamon, and a pinch of salt into the mixture and stir until thoroughly combined. Halve the dough, shape into balls, wrap in plastic wrap, and chill in the refrigerator for 30–60 minutes.

2. Preheat the oven to 375°F/190°C. Line 2 cookie sheets with baking parchment.

3. Unwrap the dough and roll out between 2 sheets of baking parchment. Stamp out cookies with a 2½-inch/6-cm fluted round cutter and put them on the prepared cookie sheets spaced well apart.

4. Bake for 10–15 minutes. Leave to cool for 5 minutes. Add the marshmallows and return to the oven and cook for 1–2 minutes. Transfer the cookies to wire racks and let stand for 30 minutes.

5. Melt the chocolate in a heatproof bowl set over a saucepan of gently simmering water. Remove from the heat and let cool. Line a cookie sheet with baking parchment. Spread the marmalade over the undersides of the uncovered cookies and place them on top of the marshmallow-covered cookies. Dip the cookies in the melted chocolate to coat, letting the excess drip back into the bowl, then place them on the cookie sheet. Put a walnut half in the center of each cookie. Let set.

Makes about 15

* 1 cup butter, softened
* scant ¾ cup superfine sugar
* 2 tsp finely grated orange rind
* 1 egg yolk, lightly beaten
* 2¼ cups all-purpose flour
* ¼ cup unsweetened cocoa powder
* ½ tsp ground cinnamon
* 30 yellow marshmallows, halved horizontally
* 10½ oz/300 g bittersweet chocolate, broken into pieces
* 4 tbsp orange marmalade
* 15 walnut halves
* salt

Tropical Fruit & Mascarpone Cream Cookie Sandwiches

1. Put the butter and sugar into a bowl and mix well with a wooden spoon, then beat in the egg yolk and passion fruit pulp. Sift together the flour and a pinch of salt into the mixture, add the mango, papaya, and dates, and stir until thoroughly combined. Shape the dough into a log, wrap in plastic wrap, and chill in the refrigerator for 30–60 minutes.

2. Meanwhile, make the mascarpone cream. Put all the ingredients in a bowl and beat with a wooden spoon until thoroughly combined and smooth. Cover the bowl with plastic wrap and chill in the refrigerator.

3. Preheat the oven to 375°F/190°C. Line 2 cookie sheets with baking parchment.

4. Unwrap the dough and cut into slices with a sharp serrated knife. Put them on the prepared cookie sheets spaced well apart.

5. Bake for 10–15 minutes, until light golden brown. Let cool on the cookie sheets for 5–10 minutes, then using a metal spatula, carefully transfer to wire racks to cool completely. When the cookies are cold spread the chilled mascarpone cream over half of them, sprinkle with the toasted coconut, and top with the remaining cookies.

Makes about 15

- 1 cup butter, softened
- scant ¾ cup superfine sugar
- 1 egg yolk, lightly beaten
- 2 tsp passion fruit pulp
- 2½ cups all-purpose flour
- ⅓ cup chopped plumped dried mango
- ⅓ cup chopped plumped dried papaya
- 3 tbsp pitted and chopped dried dates
- 3–4 tbsp shredded coconut, toasted
- salt

Mascarpone cream
- ⅓ cup mascarpone cheese
- 3 tbsp strained plain yogurt
- 7 tbsp prepared custard
- ½ tsp ground ginger

Banana & Caramel Cookies

1. Put the butter and sugar into a bowl and mix well with a wooden spoon, then beat in the egg yolk, ginger, and ginger syrup. Sift together the flour and a pinch of salt into the mixture, add the bananas, and stir until thoroughly combined. Halve the dough, shape into balls, wrap in plastic wrap, and chill in the refrigerator for 30–60 minutes.

2. Preheat the oven to 375°F/190°C. Line 2 cookie sheets with baking parchment.

3. Unwrap the dough and roll out between 2 sheets of baking parchment. Stamp out cookies with a 2½-inch/6-cm fluted round cutter and put half of them on the prepared cookie sheets spaced well apart. Place a chocolate caramel in the center of each cookie, then top with the remaining cookies, and pinch the edges of the cookie sandwiches together.

4. Bake for 10–15 minutes, until light golden brown. Let cool on the cookie sheets for 5–10 minutes, then using a metal spatula, carefully transfer to wire racks to cool completely.

Makes about 30

* 1 cup butter, softened
* scant ¾ cup superfine sugar
* 1 egg yolk, lightly beaten
  2 tbsp finely chopped preserved ginger, plus 2 tsp syrup from the jar
* 2½ cups all-purpose flour
  3 oz/85 g dried bananas, finely chopped
  15 chocolate caramel candies
* salt

98

Rich Peanut, Pineapple & Cream Cheese Cookie Sandwiches

1. Set aside half the peanuts and finely chop the remainder. Put the butter and sugar into a bowl and mix well with a wooden spoon, then beat in the egg yolk. Sift together the flour, allspice, chopped peanuts, and a pinch of salt into the mixture and stir until thoroughly combined. Halve the dough, shape into balls, wrap in plastic wrap, and chill in the refrigerator for 30–60 minutes.

2. Preheat the oven to 375°F/190°C. Line 2 cookie sheets with baking parchment.

3. Unwrap the dough and roll out between 2 sheets of baking parchment. Sprinkle evenly with the reserved peanuts and lightly roll with the rolling pin. Stamp out cookies with a 2–2½-inch/5–6-cm fluted round cutter and put them on the prepared cookie sheets spaced well apart.

4. Bake for 10–15 minutes, until light golden brown. Let cool on the cookie sheets for 5–10 minutes, then using a metal spatula, carefully transfer to wire racks to cool completely.

5. For the filling, beat together the cream and cream cheese until thick and smooth. Fold in the candied pineapple. Spread the mixture over the undersides of half the cookies and top with the remaining cookies, peanut side uppermost.

Makes about 15

6 tbsp salted peanuts
1 cup butter, softened
scant ¾ cup superfine sugar
1 egg yolk, lightly beaten
2½ cups all-purpose flour
½ tsp ground allspice
salt

Cream cheese filling
3 tbsp heavy cream
⅓ cup cream cheese
½ cup chopped candied pineapple

Chocolate Mint Cookie Sandwiches

1. Put the butter and sugar into a bowl and mix well with a wooden spoon, then beat in the egg yolk and vanilla extract. Sift together the flour, unsweetened cocoa powder, and a pinch of salt into the mixture, add the cherries, and stir until thoroughly combined. Halve the dough, shape into balls, wrap in plastic wrap, and chill in the refrigerator for 30–60 minutes.

2. Preheat the oven to 375°F/190°C. Line 2 cookie sheets with baking parchment.

3. Unwrap the dough and roll out between 2 sheets of baking parchment. Stamp out cookies with a 2½-in/6-cm plain square cutter and put them on the prepared cookie sheets spaced well apart.

4. Bake for 10–15 minutes, until firm. Immediately place an after-dinner mint on top of half the cookies, then cover with the remaining cookies. Press down gently and let cool.

5. Melt the semisweet chocolate in a heatproof bowl set over a saucepan of gently simmering water. Remove from the heat and let cool. Put the cookies on a wire rack over a sheet of baking parchment. Spoon the semisweet chocolate over them, then tap the rack to level the surface, and let set. Melt the white chocolate in a heatproof bowl set over a saucepan of barely simmering water. Remove from the heat and let cool. Pipe or drizzle it over the cookies, then let set.

Makes about 15

* 1 cup butter, softened
* scant ¾ cup superfine sugar
* 1 egg yolk, lightly beaten
* 2 tsp vanilla extract
* 2¼ cups all-purpose flour
  ½ cup unsweetened cocoa powder
  ⅓ cup candied cherries, finely chopped
  15 after-dinner mints
* salt

Chocolate coating
4 oz/115 g semisweet chocolate, broken into pieces
2 oz/55 g white chocolate, broken into pieces

Ice Cream Cookie Sandwiches

1. Put the butter and sugar into a bowl and mix well with a wooden spoon, then beat in the egg yolk, ginger, and ginger syrup. Sift together the flour, unsweetened cocoa powder, cinnamon, and a pinch of salt into the mixture and stir until thoroughly combined. Halve the dough, shape into balls, wrap in plastic wrap, and chill in the refrigerator for 30–60 minutes.

2. Preheat the oven to 375°F/190°C. Line 2 cookie sheets with baking parchment.

3. Unwrap the dough and roll out between 2 sheets of baking parchment. Stamp out cookies with a 2½-inch/6-cm fluted round cutter and put them on the prepared cookie sheets spaced well apart.

4. Bake for 10–15 minutes, until light golden brown. Let cool on the cookie sheets for 5–10 minutes, then using a metal spatula, carefully transfer to wire racks to cool completely.

5. Remove the ice cream from the freezer about 15 minutes before serving to let it soften. Put a generous scoop of ice cream on half the cookies and top with the remaining cookies. Press together gently so that the filling spreads to the edges. If not serving immediately, wrap the cookies individually in foil, and store in the freezer.

Makes about 30

* 1 cup butter, softened
* scant ¾ cup golden superfine sugar
* 1 egg yolk, lightly beaten
* 2 tbsp finely chopped preserved ginger, plus 2 tsp syrup from the jar
* 2¼ cups all-purpose flour
* ¼ cup unsweetened cocoa powder
* ½ tsp ground cinnamon
* 2 cups vanilla, chocolate, or coffee ice cream
* salt

allspice
  cinnamon & caramel cookies 38
  rich peanut, pineapple & cream cheese
    cookie sandwiches 216
almonds
  almond cookies with green tea cream 189
  almond crunchies 58
  almond & raspberry jam drops 22
  apple suns & pear stars 165
  chocolate & apricot cookies 144
  Neapolitan cookies 80
  peach, pear & plum cookies 180
  pistachio & almond cookies 88
  Turkish delight cookies 106
alphabet cookies 68
amaretto: chocolate & apricot cookies 144
angelica: fennel & angelica cookies 73
apple pie spice
  apple & spice cookies 190
  apple suns & pear stars 165
  mixed fruit cookies 142
  traditional Easter cookies 130
apples
  apple & spice cookies 190
  apple suns & pear stars 165
  mixed fruit cookies 142
apricots
  apricot & pecan cookies 86
  chocolate & apricot cookies 144

bananas
  banana & caramel cookies 214
  banana & raisin cookies 153
basic cookie dough mix 10
biscotti 82
blueberries
  blueberry & cranberry cinnamon cookies 171
  blueberry & orange cookies 168
  Thanksgiving cookies 122
butterfly cookies 112

candied peel
  almond & raspberry jam drops 22
  chewy candied fruit cookies 50
  Easter nest cookies 127

traditional Easter cookies 130
cappuccino cookies 91
caramel glaze cookies 32
Caribbean cookies 121
cashew nuts
  cashew & poppy seed cookies 74
  crunchy nut & honey sandwich cookies 202
  papaya & cashew nut cookies 177
chamomile cookies 92
cherries: double choc cookies 14
cherries, candied
  cherry & chocolate diamonds 154
  chewy candied fruit cookies 50
  chocolate mint cookie sandwiches 219
  Easter nest cookies 127
  traffic lights 26
chewy candied fruit cookies 50
chocolate
  cappuccino cookies 91
  cherry & chocolate diamonds 154
  choco mint stars 20
  chocolate & apricot cookies 144
  chocolate buttons 103
  chocolate chip & cinnamon cookies 56
  chocolate, date & pecan nut pinwheels 37
  chocolate dominoes 110
  chocolate fudge squares 16
  chocolate & ginger checkerboard cookies 98
  chocolate mint cookie sandwiches 219
  chocolate & orange cookie sandwiches 208
  chocolate spread & hazelnut drops 52
  chocolate sprinkle cookies 46
  Christmas bells 136
  clubs & spades 207
  double choc cookies 14
  double heart cookies 124
  Easter bunny cookies 128
  golden hazelnut cookies 85
  Halloween spider's web cookies 133
  hearts & diamonds 204
  ice cream cookie sandwiches 220
  lemon & lime cookies 159
  marshmallow daisies 40
  marshmallow s'mores 210
  mega chip cookies 19

melt-in-the-middles 44
mint cookies with white chocolate ganache
  186
Neapolitan cookies 80
orange & chocolate fingers 25
plum & white chocolate cookies 174
sticky ginger cookies 28
sugared hearts 109
Thanksgiving cookies 122
Christmas angels 134
Christmas bells 136
Christmas tree decorations 139
cinnamon
  apple & spice cookies 190
  blueberry & cranberry cinnamon cookies 171
  cashew & poppy seed cookies 74
  chocolate chip & cinnamon cookies 56
  Christmas bells 136
  cinnamon & caramel cookies 38
  cinnamon & orange crisps 94
  date & lemon spirals 172
  ice cream cookie sandwiches 220
  marshmallow s'mores 210
  number crunchers 70
  snickerdoodles 62
  spicy cinnamon cookies 49
classic saffron cookies 118
cloves
  number crunchers 70
  spicy cinnamon cookies 49
clubs & spades 207
coconut
  Caribbean cookies 121
  choco mint stars 20
  chocolate dominoes 110
  Christmas angels 134
  coconut & cranberry cookies 166
  mango, coconut & ginger cookies 160
  melt-in-the-middles 44
  strawberry pinks 162
  traffic lights 26
  tropical fruit & mascarpone cream cookie
    sandwiches 213
  Turkish delight cookies 106
coffee

cappuccino cookies 91
  coffee cream & walnut cookies 198
  double heart cookies 124
  walnut & coffee cookies 79
corn syrup
  clubs & spades 207
  pineapple & ginger creams 201
cranberries
  blueberry & cranberry cinnamon cookies 171
  coconut & cranberry cookies 166
  Thanksgiving cookies 122
cream
  chocolate fudge squares 16
  mint cookies with white chocolate ganache 186
  rich peanut, pineapple & cream cheese cookie sandwiches 216
cream cheese
  almond cookies with green tea cream 189
  blueberry & orange cookies 168
  hearts & diamonds 204
  rich peanut, pineapple & cream cheese cookie sandwiches 216
  tropical fruit & mascarpone cream cookie sandwiches 213
crunchy nut & honey sandwich cookies 202
currants
  classic saffron cookies 118
  traditional Easter cookies 130

dates
  chocolate, date & pecan nut pinwheels 37
  date & lemon spirals 172
  tropical fruit & mascarpone cream cookie sandwiches 213
double choc cookies 14
double heart cookies 124

Easter bunny cookies 128
Easter nest cookies 127

fennel & angelica cookies 73
figs: walnut & fig pinwheels 150
flower gems 61

ginger
  apple suns & pear stars 165
  banana & caramel cookies 214
  chocolate & ginger checkerboard cookies 98
  Easter bunny cookies 128
  ice cream cookie sandwiches 220
  mango, coconut & ginger cookies 160
  number crunchers 70
  orange & chocolate fingers 25
  peanut partners 43
  pineapple & ginger creams 201
  sticky ginger cookies 28
  tropical fruit & mascarpone cream cookie sandwiches 213
golden hazelnut cookies 85
grapefruit & apple mint cookies 156

Halloween spider's web cookies 133
hazelnuts
  chocolate spread & hazelnut drops 52
  golden hazelnut cookies 85
  oaty raisin & hazelnut cookies 178
hearts & diamonds 204
honey
  crunchy nut & honey sandwich cookies 202
  date & lemon spirals 172

ice cream cookie sandwiches 220
iced stars 100

jam
  almond & raspberry jam drops 22
  jam rings 184
  marshmallow daisies 40
  peach, pear & plum cookies 180
  strawberry pinks 162
jelly
  hearts & diamonds 204
  peanut butter & grape jelly cookies 31

lavender cookies 64
lemons
  biscotti 82
  caramel glaze cookies 32
  Christmas bells 136
  date & lemon spirals 172

Easter nest cookies 127
  lemon & lime cookies 159
  lemon & sesame seed cookies 76
  orange & lemon cookies 148
  peanut partners 43
limes
  Caribbean cookies 121
  lemon & lime cookies 159
  margarita cookies 115
  papaya & cashew nut cookies 177
  peach daiquiri cookies 116

macadamia nuts
  blueberry & orange cookies 168
  chewy candied fruit cookies 50
  crunchy nut & honey sandwich cookies 202
  number crunchers 70
malt: butterfly cookies 112
mangoes
  mango, coconut & ginger cookies 160
  tropical fruit & mascarpone cream cookie sandwiches 213
maple syrup: chewy candied fruit cookies 50
margarita cookies 115
marshmallows
  Easter bunny cookies 128
  marshmallow daisies 40
  marshmallow s'mores 210
  Turkish delight cookies 106
mega chip cookies 19
melt-in-the-middles 44
mint
  grapefruit & apple mint cookies 156
  walnut & fig pinwheels 150
  see also peppermint
mixed fruit cookies 142

name cookies 104
Neapolitan cookies 80
number crunchers 70
nutmeg
  snickerdoodles 62
  spicy cinnamon cookies 49

oaty raisin & hazelnut cookies 178

oranges
  apricot & pecan cookies 86
  banana & raisin cookies 153
  blueberry & orange cookies 168
  chocolate chip & cinnamon cookies 56
  chocolate, date & pecan nut pinwheels 37
  chocolate & ginger checkerboard cookies 98
  chocolate & orange cookie sandwiches 208
  cinnamon & orange crisps 94
  margarita cookies 115
  marshmallow s'mores 210
  mixed fruit cookies 142
  name cookies 104
  oaty raisin & hazelnut cookies 178
  orange & chocolate fingers 25
  orange & lemon cookies 148
  rum & raisin cookies with orange filling 195
  Thanksgiving cookies 122

papaya
  melt-in-the-middles 44
  papaya & cashew nut cookies 177
  tropical fruit & mascarpone cream cookie
    sandwiches 213
passion fruit
  Christmas angels 134
  tropical fruit & mascarpone cream cookie
    sandwiches 213
peaches
  chewy candied fruit cookies 50
  peach daiquiri cookies 116
  peach, pear & plum cookies 180
peanuts
  peanut butter & grape jelly cookies 31
  peanut partners 43
  rich peanut, pineapple & cream cheese
    cookie sandwiches 216
pears
  apple suns & pear stars 165
  mixed fruit cookies 142
  peach, pear & plum cookies 180
  pear & mint cookies 34
  pear & pistachio cookies 147
pecan nuts
  apricot & pecan cookies 86

chocolate, date & pecan nut pinwheels 37
snickerdoodles 62
peppermint
  choco mint stars 20
  chocolate mint cookie sandwiches 219
  Halloween spider's web cookies 133
  mint cookies with white chocolate ganache
    186
  pear & mint cookies 34
pine nuts
  blueberry & cranberry cinnamon cookies 171
  crunchy nut & honey sandwich cookies 202
pineapple
  pineapple & ginger creams 201
  rich peanut, pineapple & cream cheese
    cookie sandwiches 216
pistachios
  biscotti 82
  pear & pistachio cookies 147
  pistachio & almond cookies 88
  Turkish delight cookies 106
plums
  peach, pear & plum cookies 180
  plum & white chocolate cookies 174
  plums & vanilla cream cookies 192
prunes: mixed fruit cookies 142
pudding mix
  almond cookies with green tea cream 189
  apple & spice cookies 190
  plums & vanilla cream cookies 192
  tropical fruit & mascarpone cream cookie
    sandwiches 213

raisins
  banana & raisin cookies 153
  oaty raisin & hazelnut cookies 178
  rum & raisin cookies with orange filling 195
red currant & pastry cream cookies 196
rich peanut, pineapple & cream cheese cookie
    sandwiches 216
rose flower cookies 67
rum
  banana & raisin cookies 153
  Caribbean cookies 121
  peach daiquiri cookies 116

rum & raisin cookies with orange filling 195

saffron: classic saffron cookies 118
seeds, edible
  alphabet cookies 68
  cashew & poppy seed cookies 74
  fennel & angelica cookies 73
  lemon & sesame seed cookies 76
snickerdoodles 62
spicy cinnamon cookies 49
sticky ginger cookies 28
strawberry pinks 162
sugared hearts 109

tea
  almond cookies with green tea cream 189
  chamomile cookies 92
  flower gems 61
  walnut & fig pinwheels 150
Thanksgiving cookies 122
traditional Easter cookies 130
traffic lights 26
tropical fruit & mascarpone cream cookie
    sandwiches 213
Turkish delight cookies 106

walnuts
  coffee cream & walnut cookies 198
  marshmallow s'mores 210
  spicy cinnamon cookies 49
  walnut & coffee cookies 79
  walnut & fig pinwheels 150

yogurt
  pineapple & ginger creams 201
tropical fruit & mascarpone cream cookie
    sandwiches 213